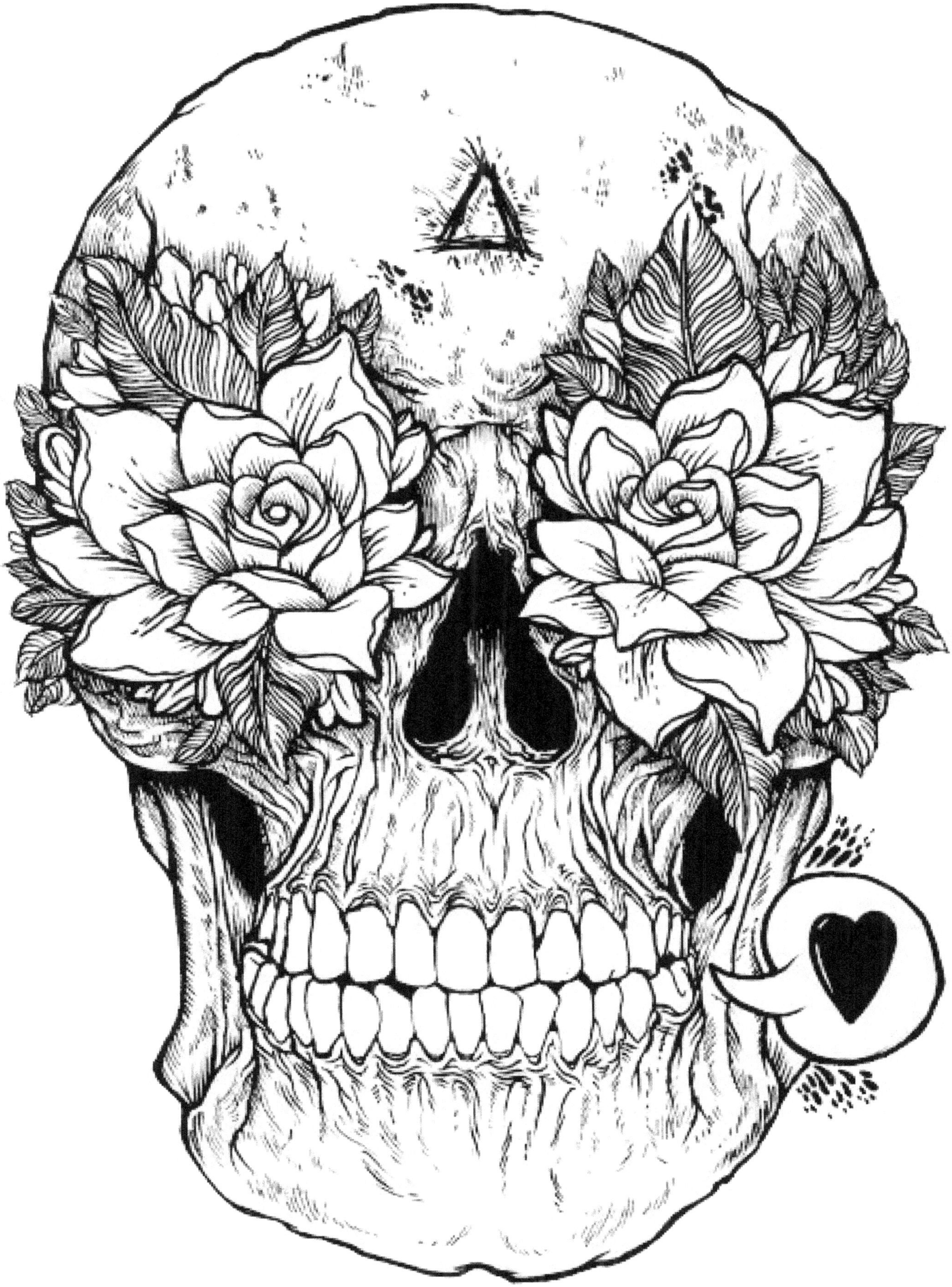

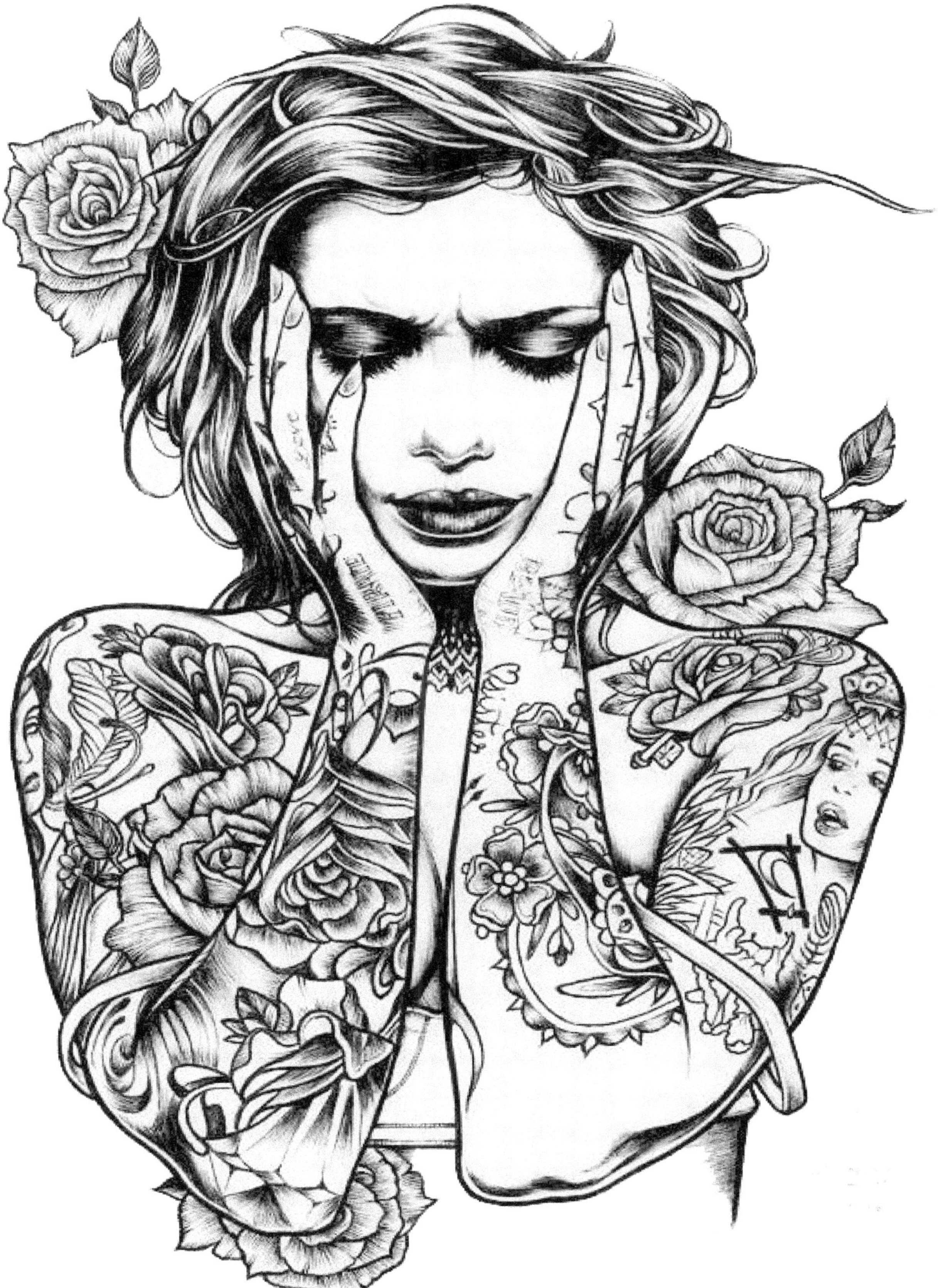

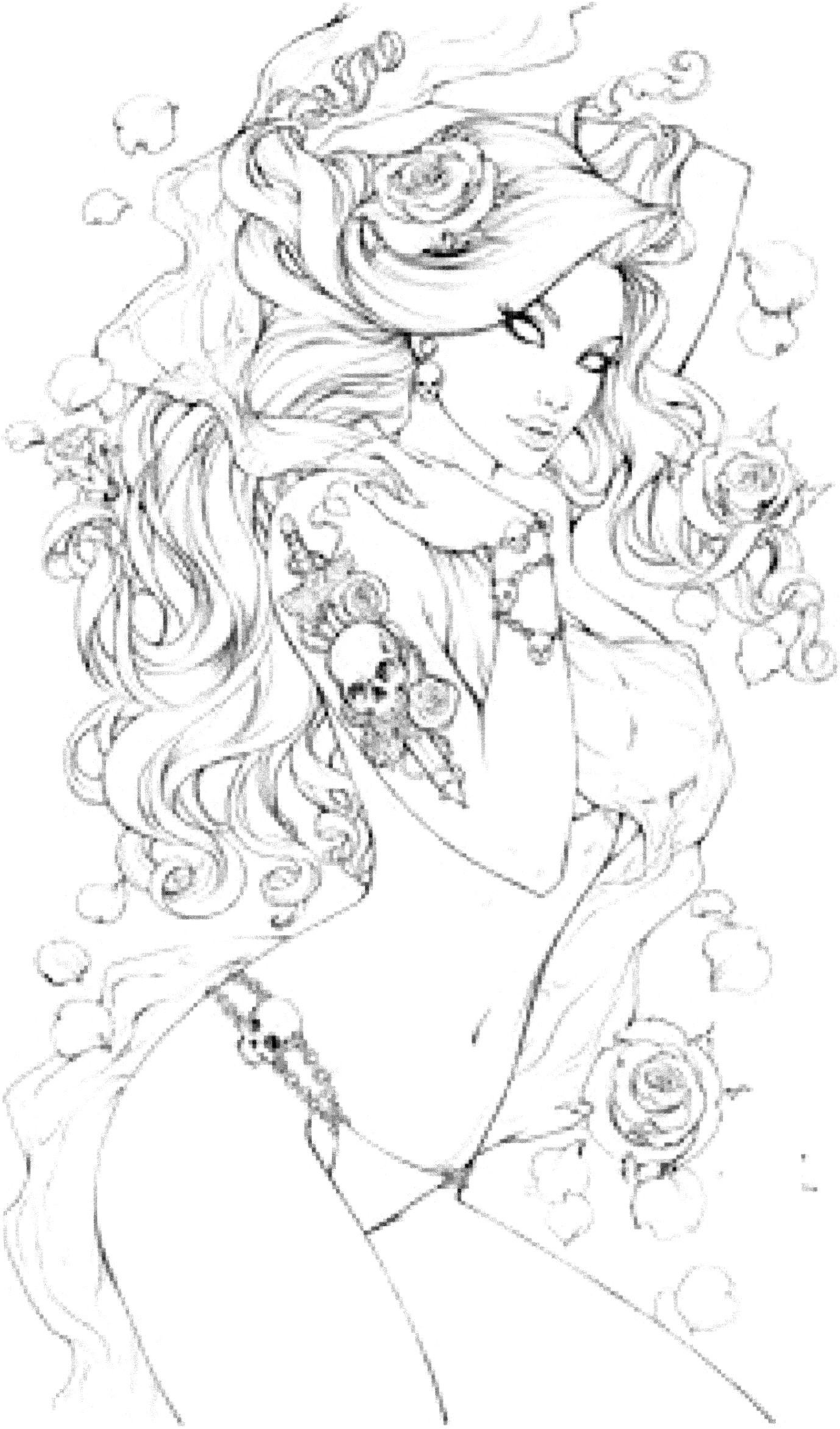

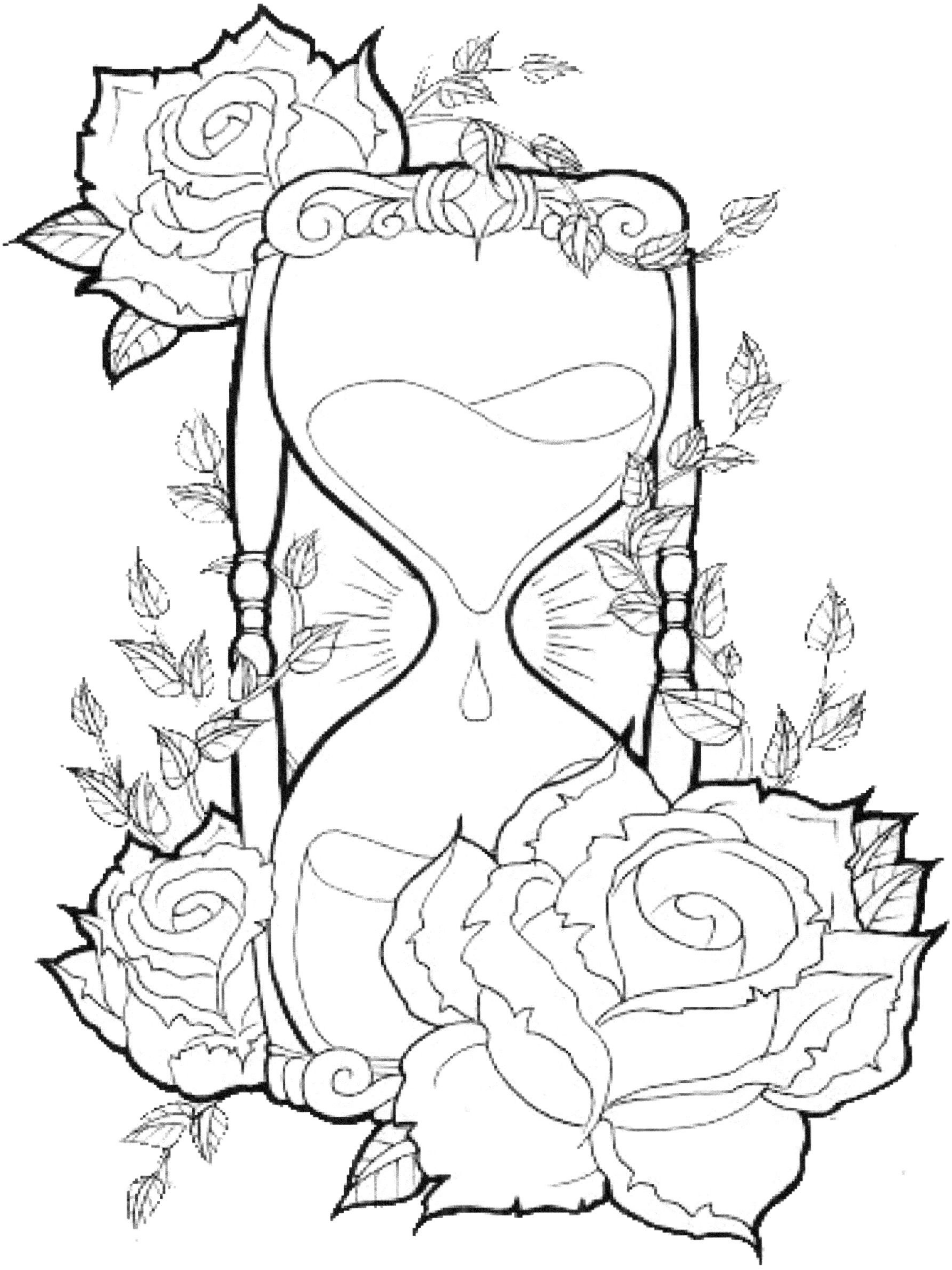

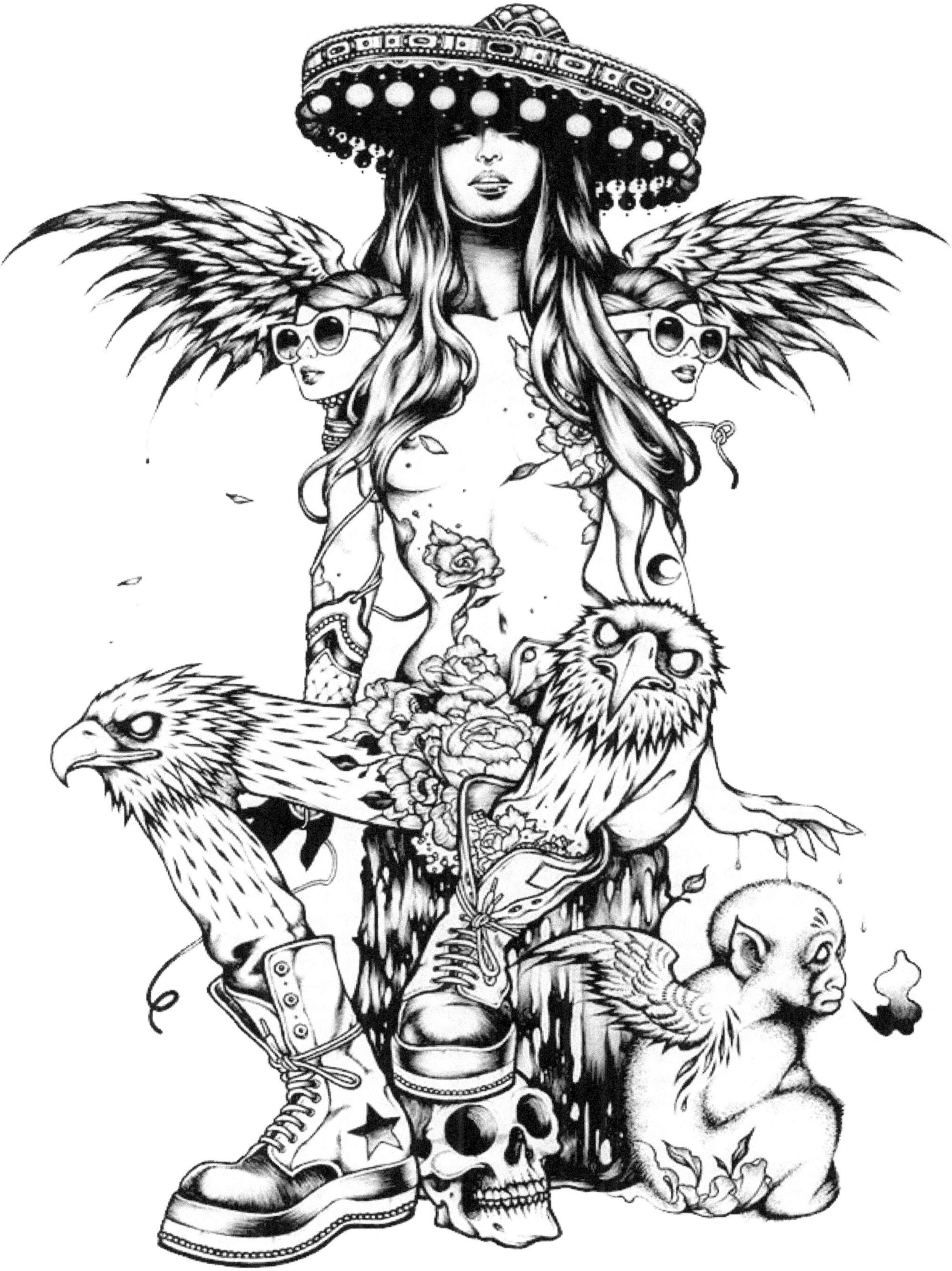

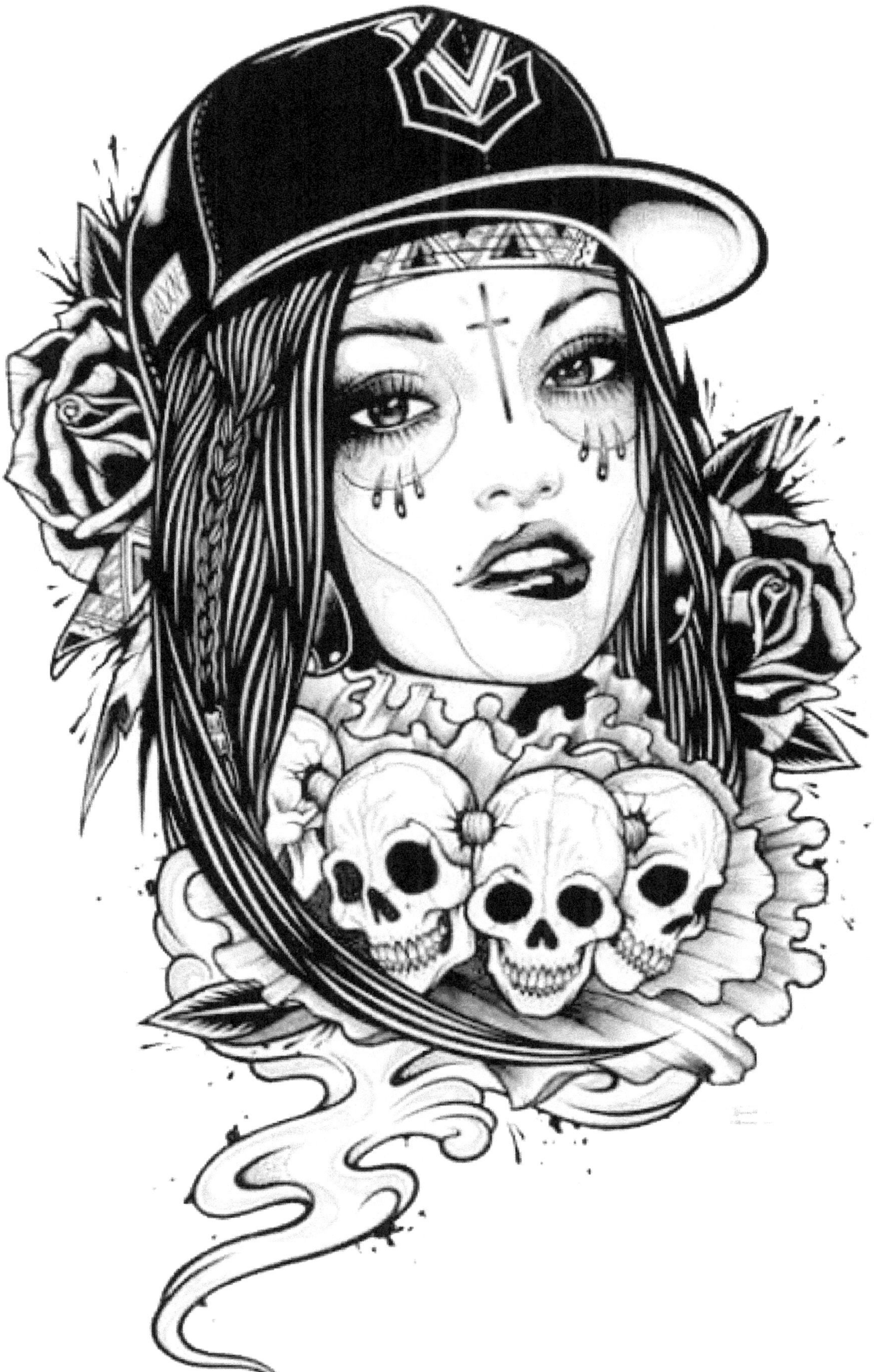

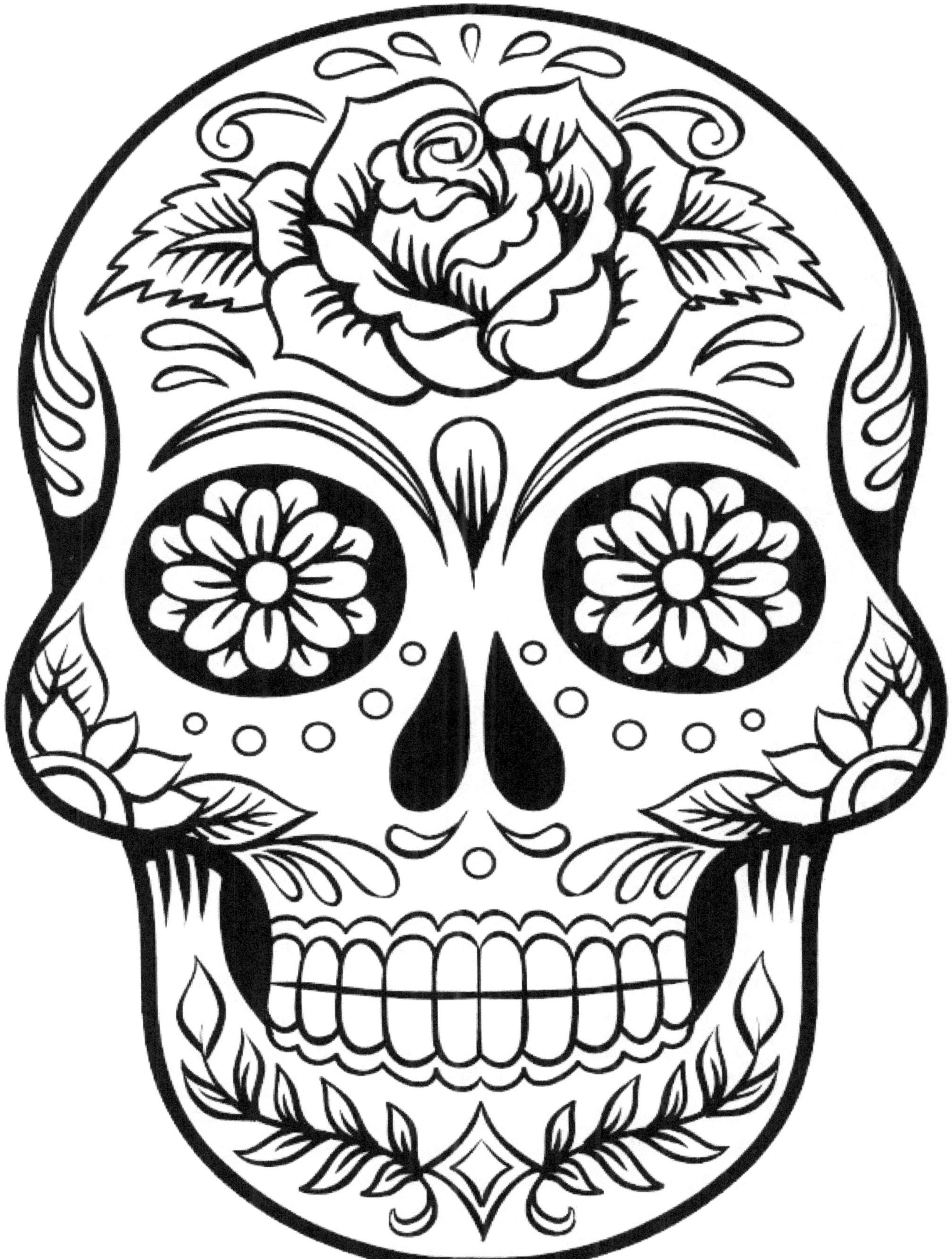

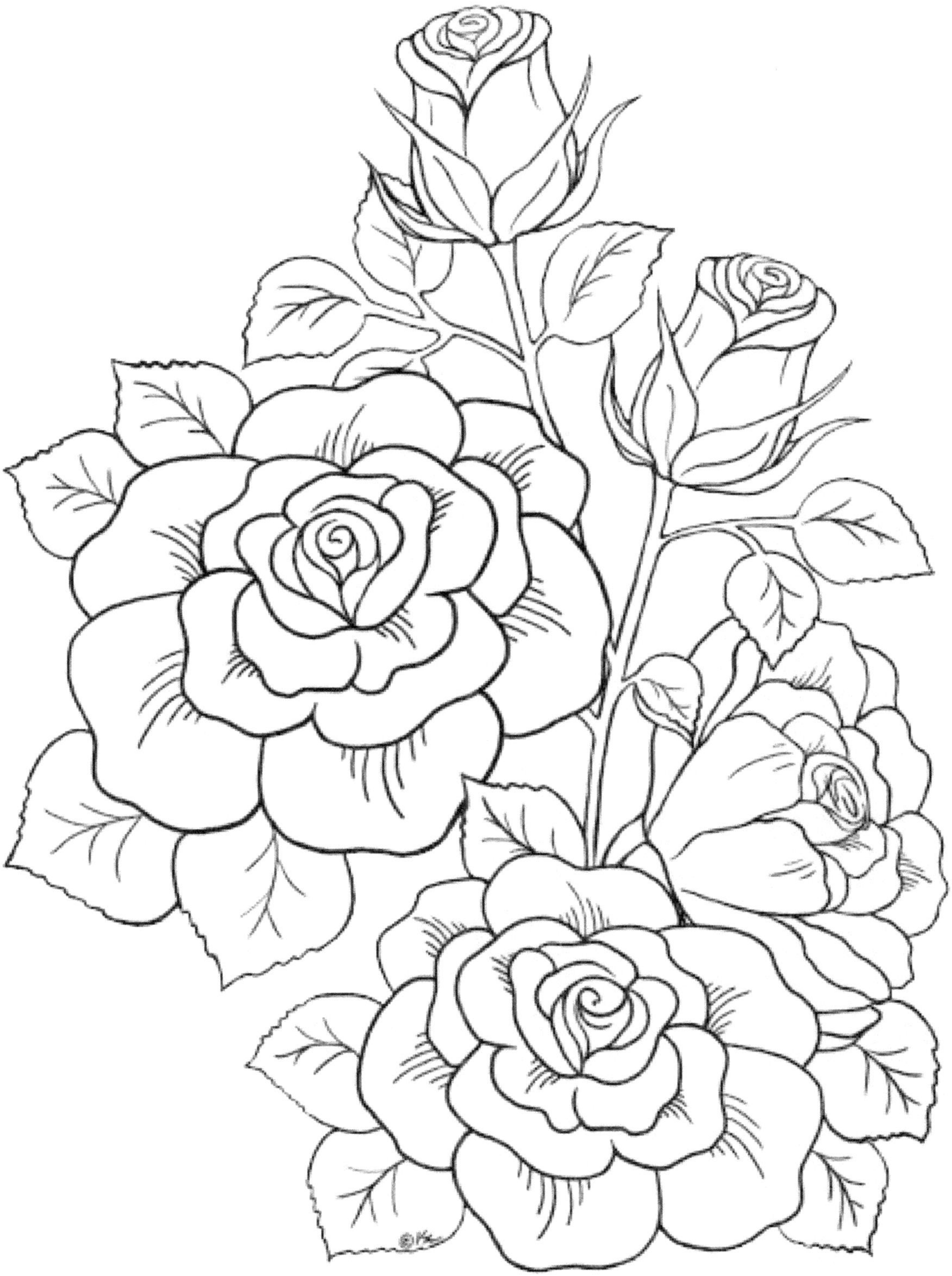

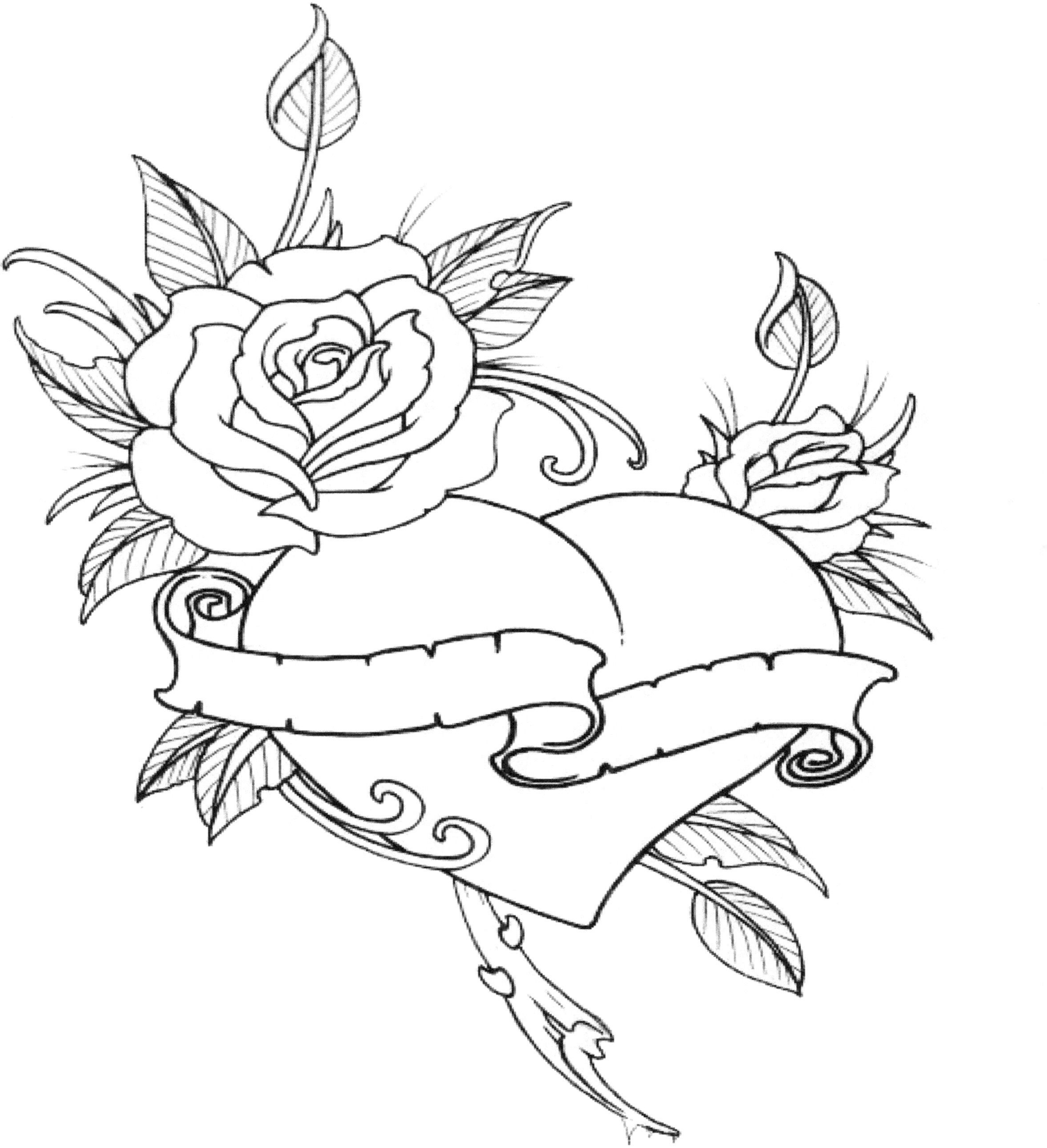

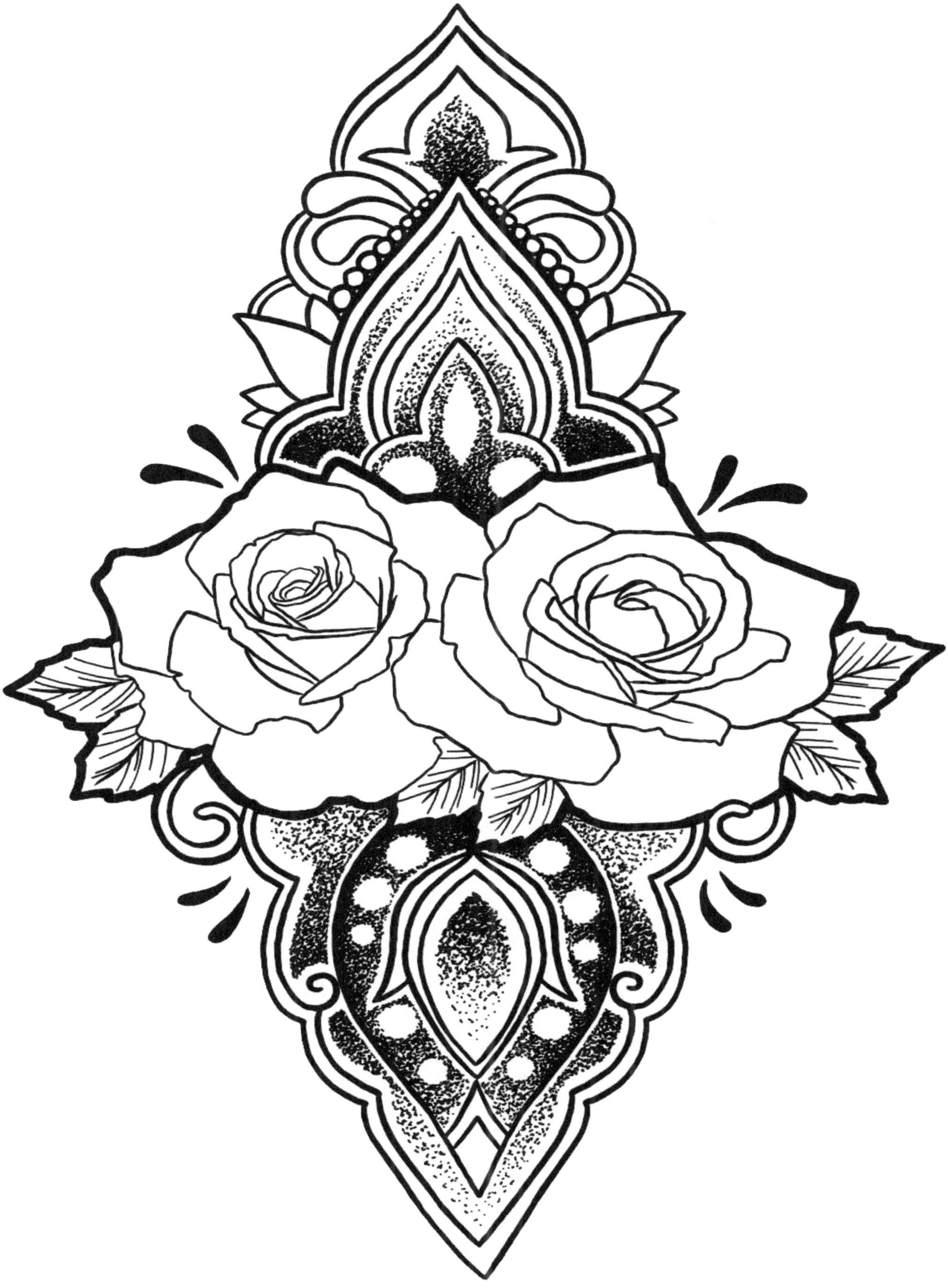

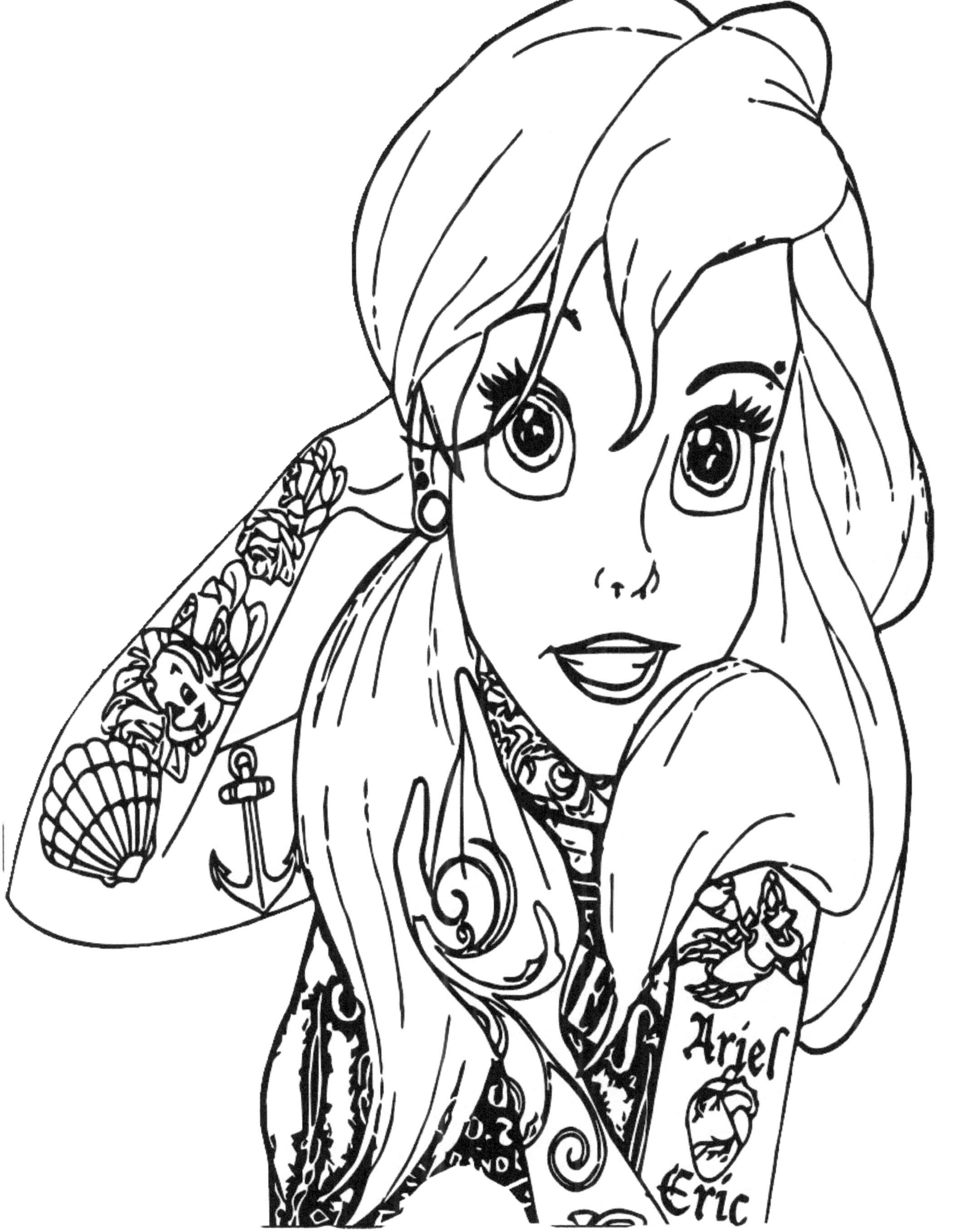
Ariel
Eric

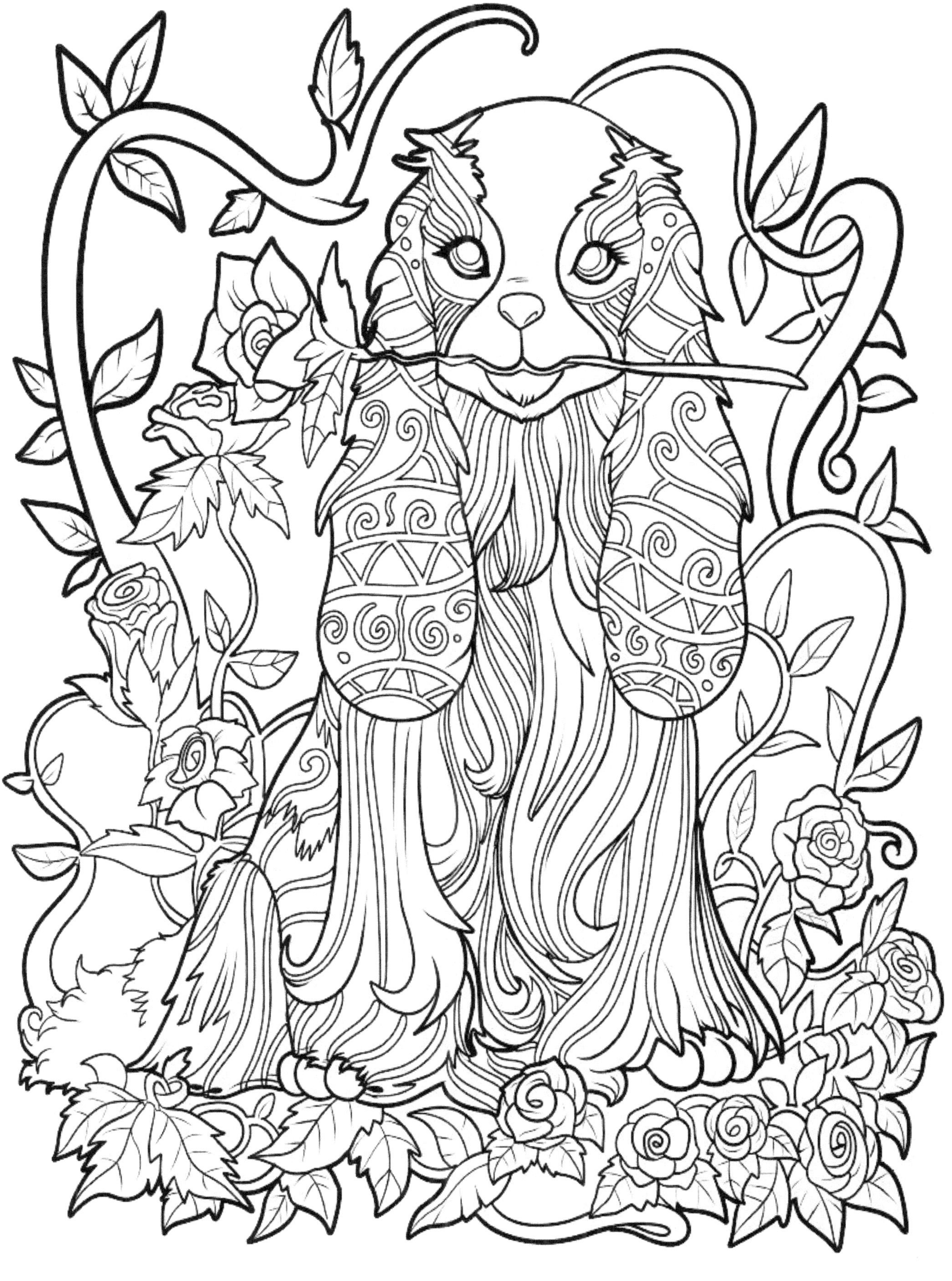

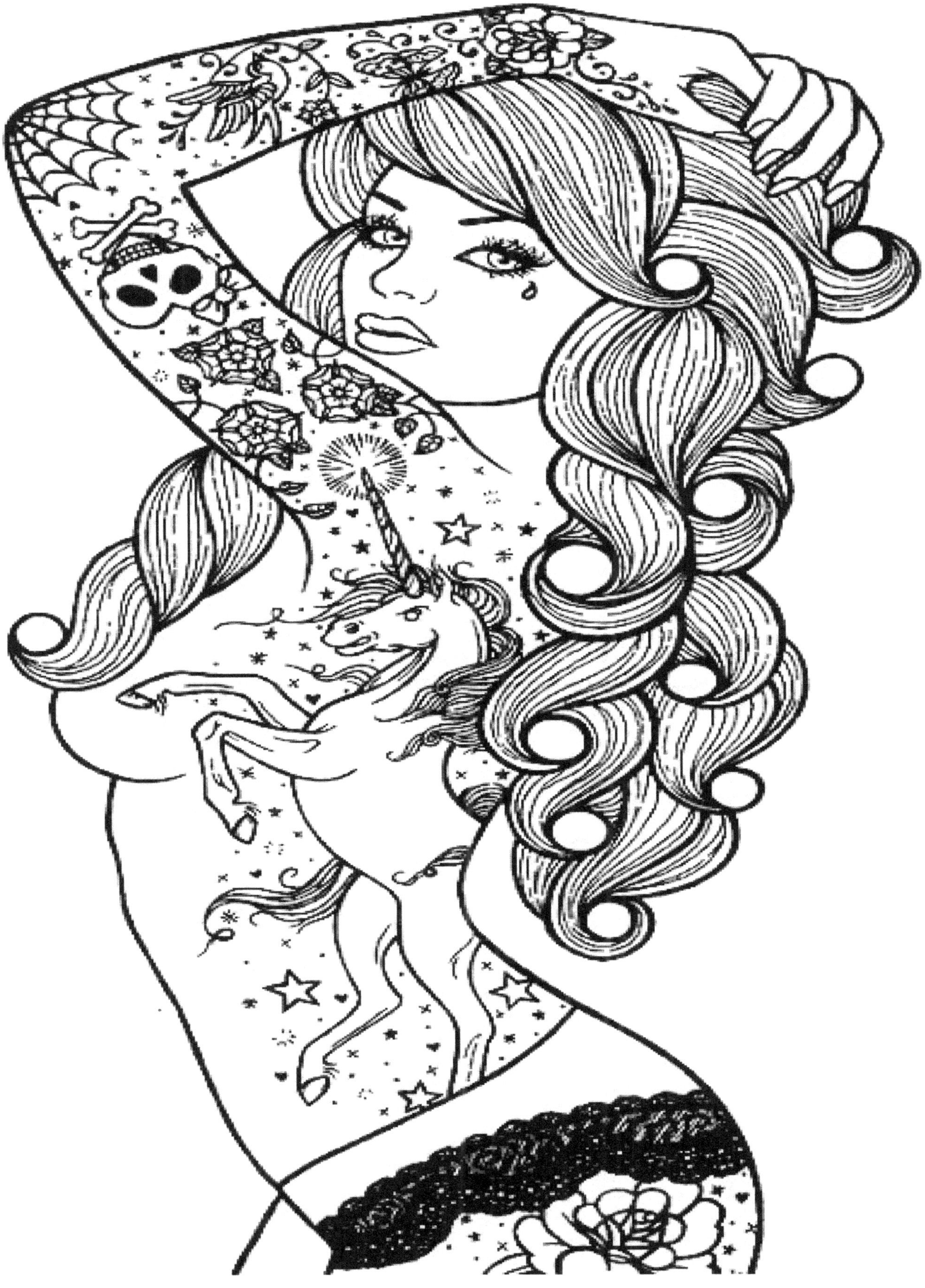

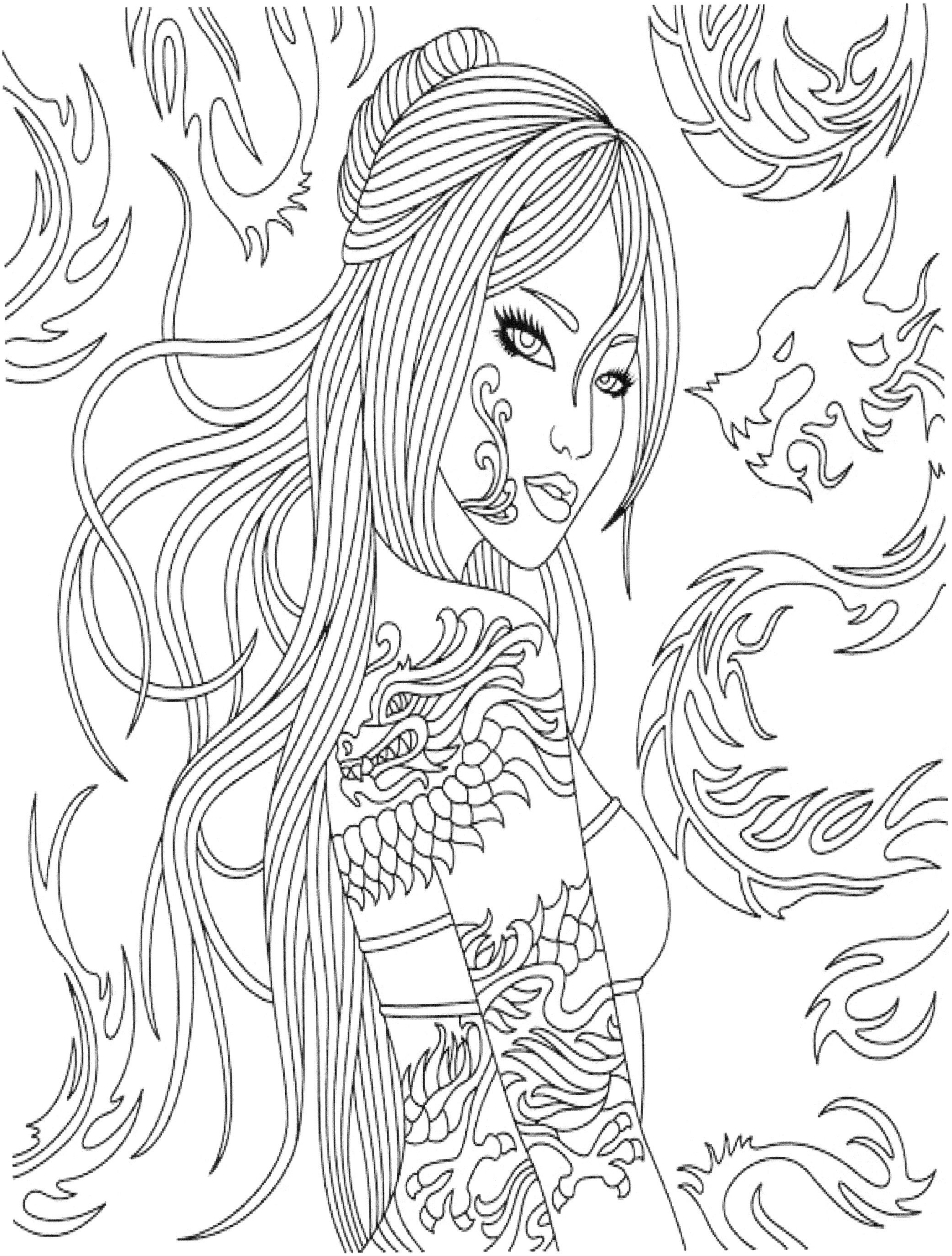

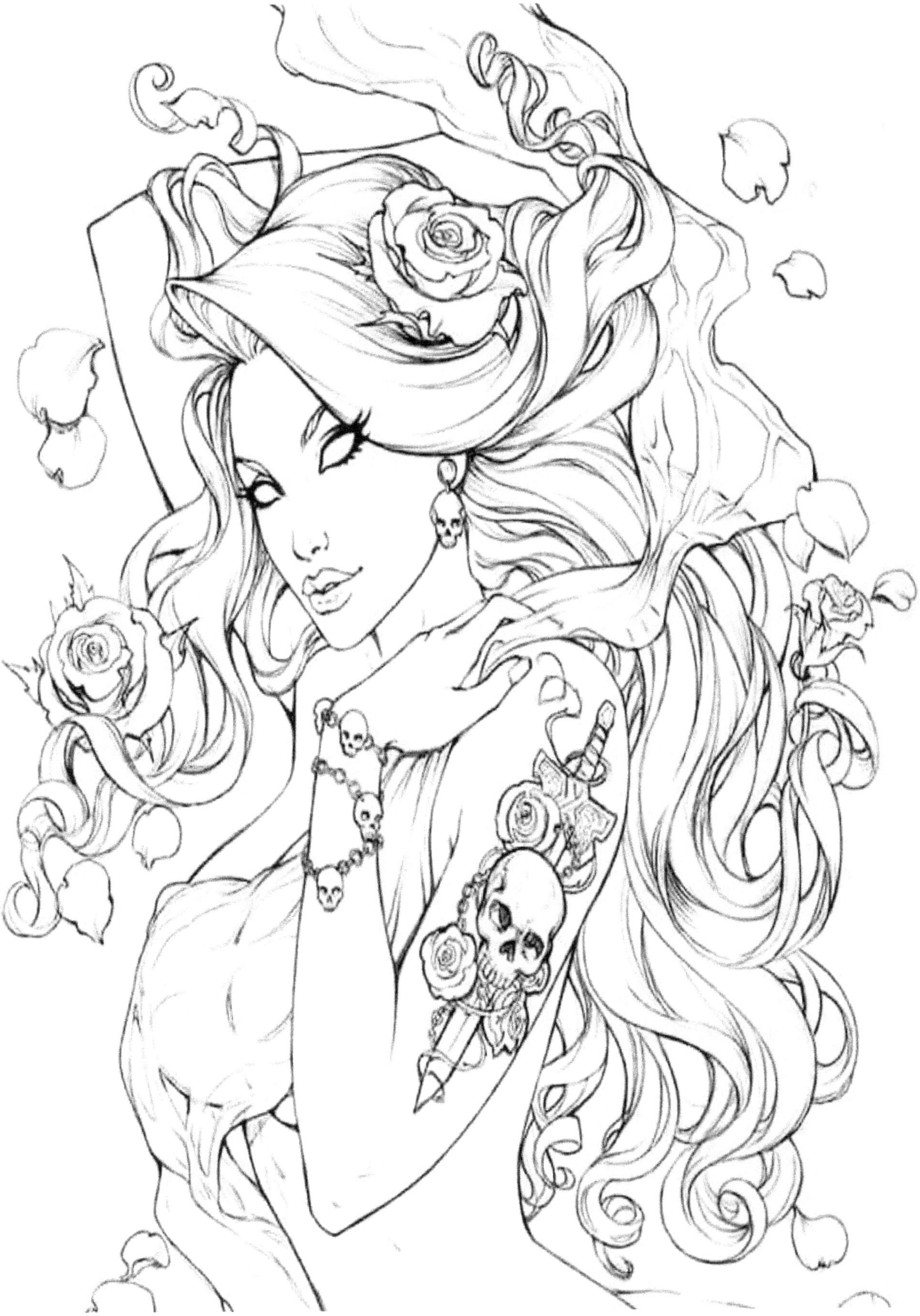

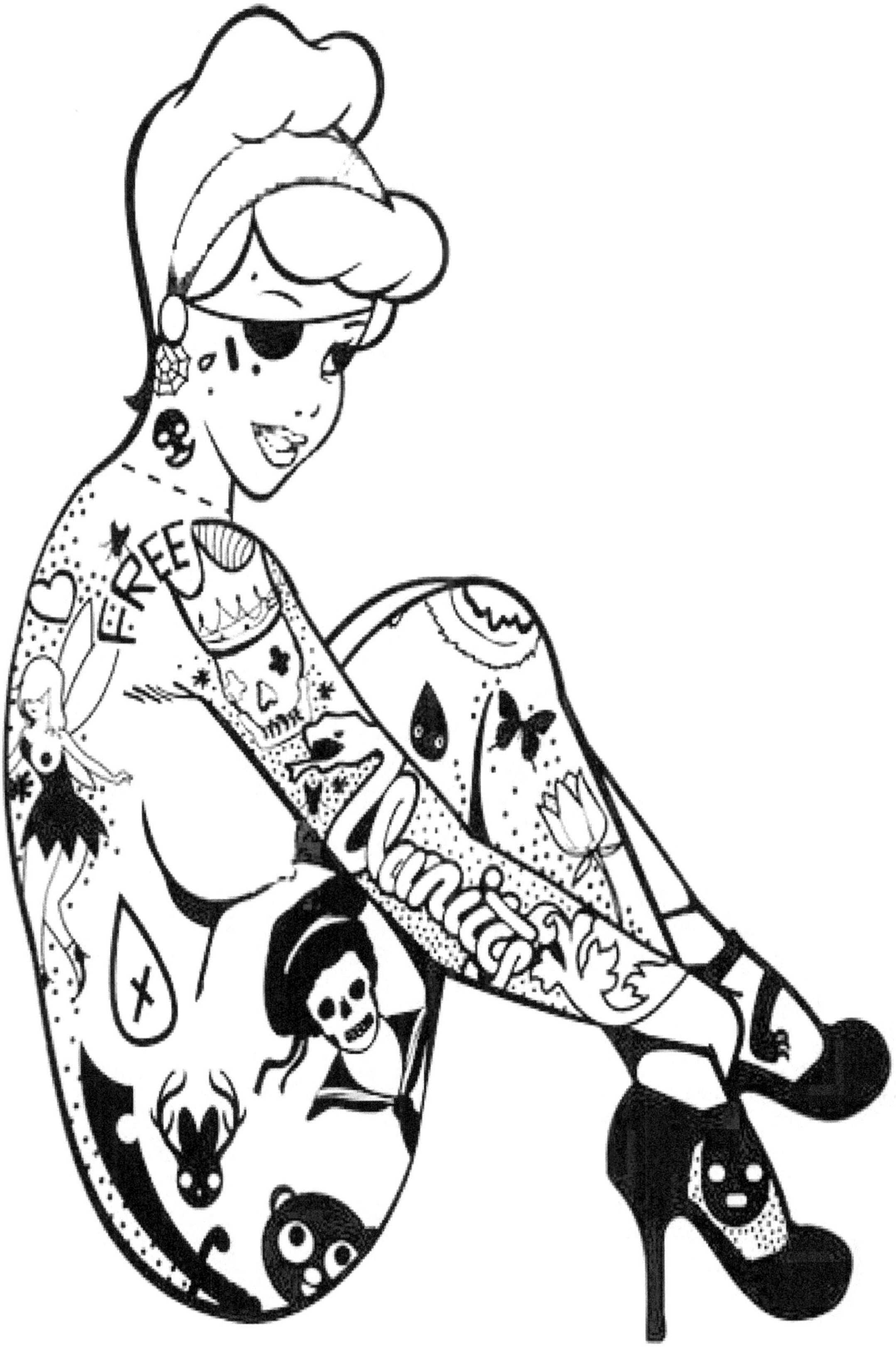
FREE

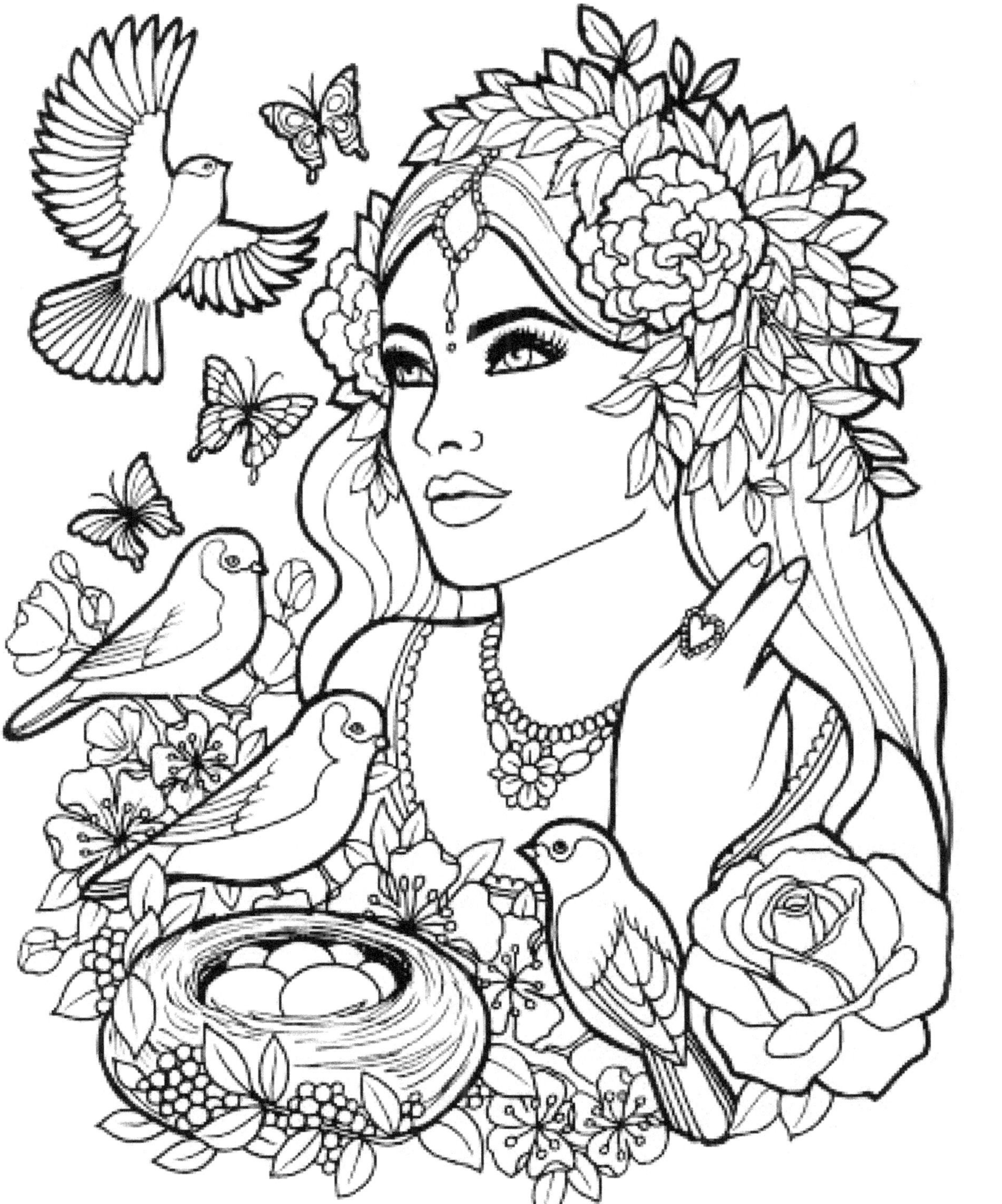

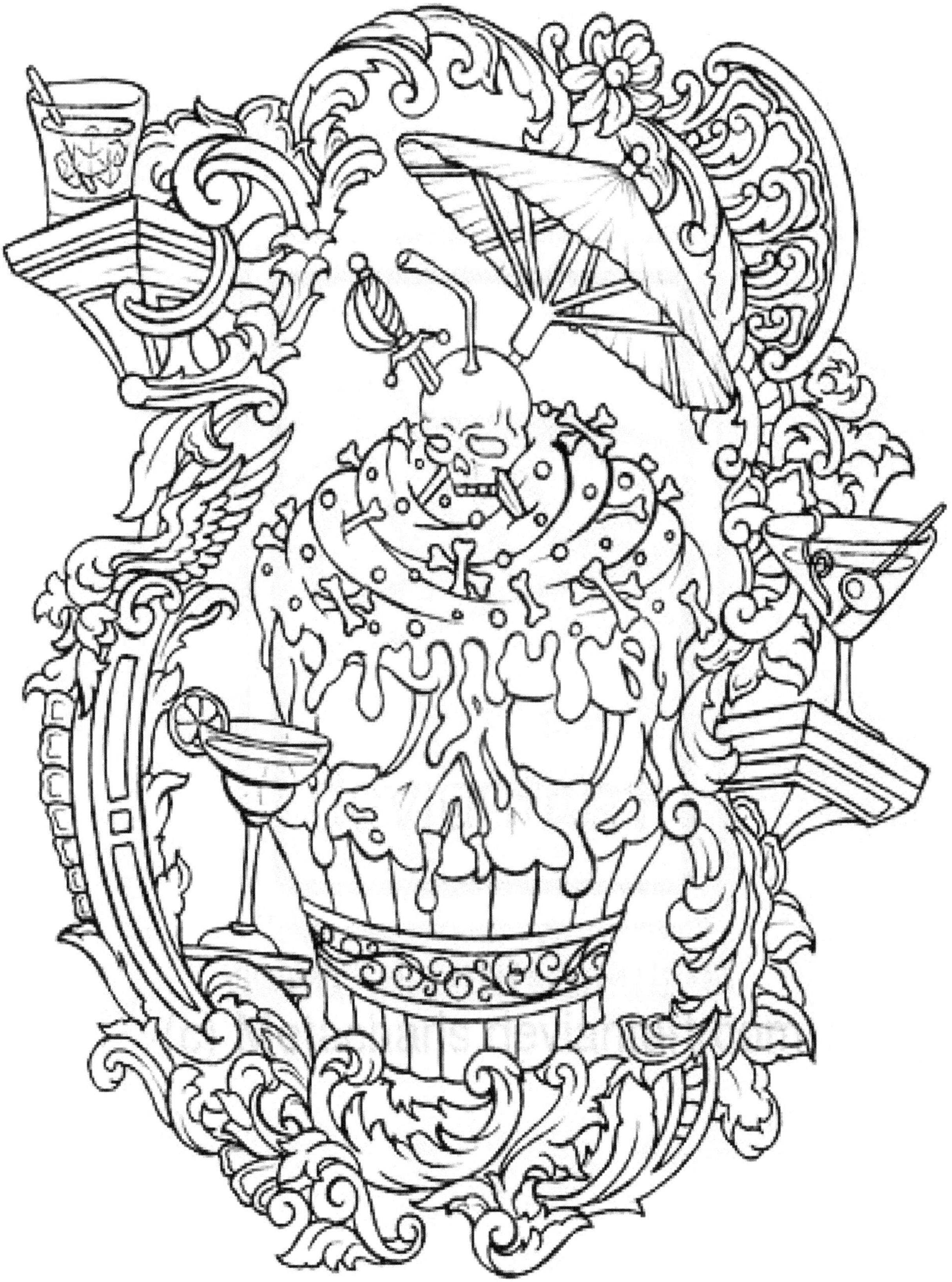

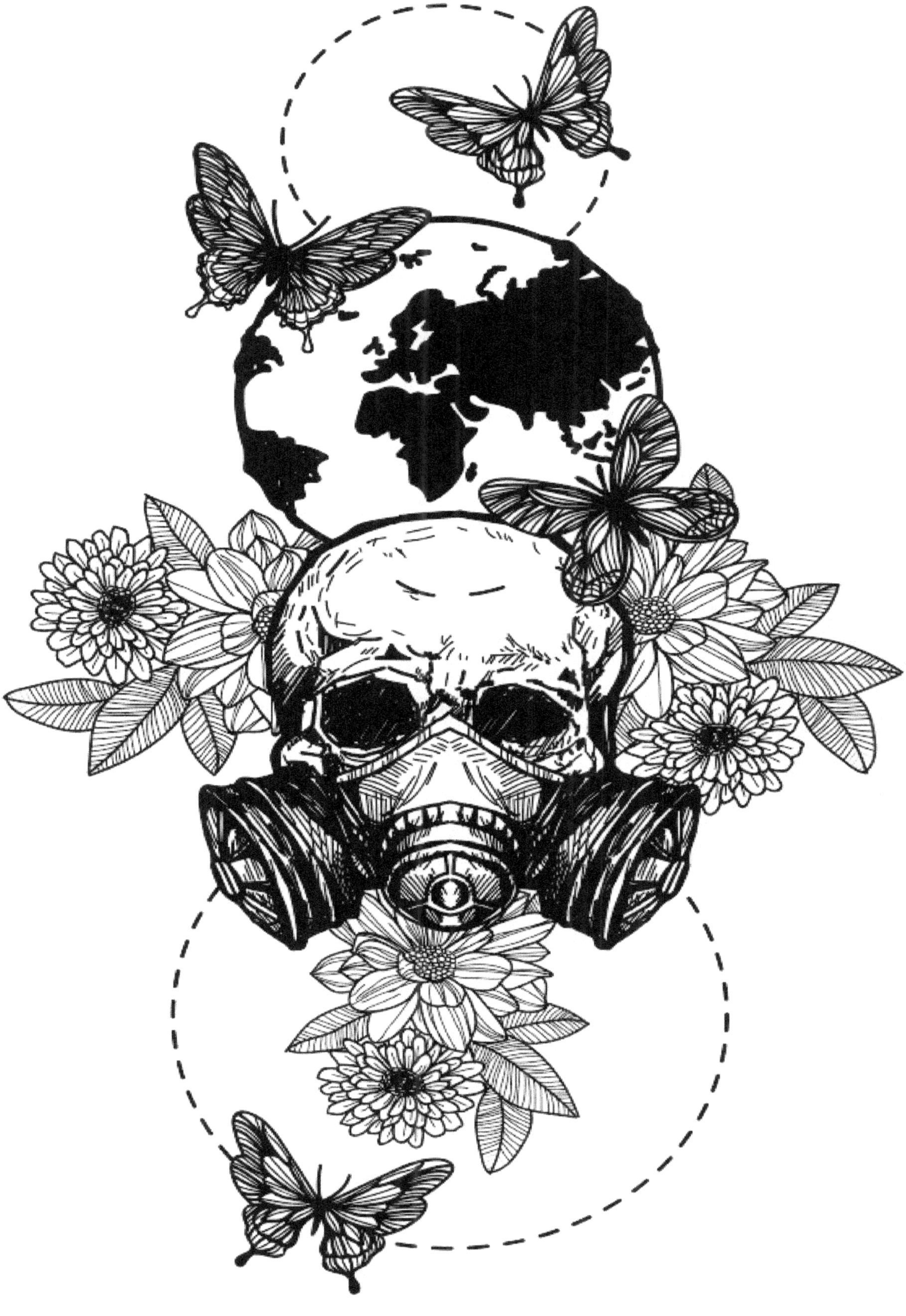

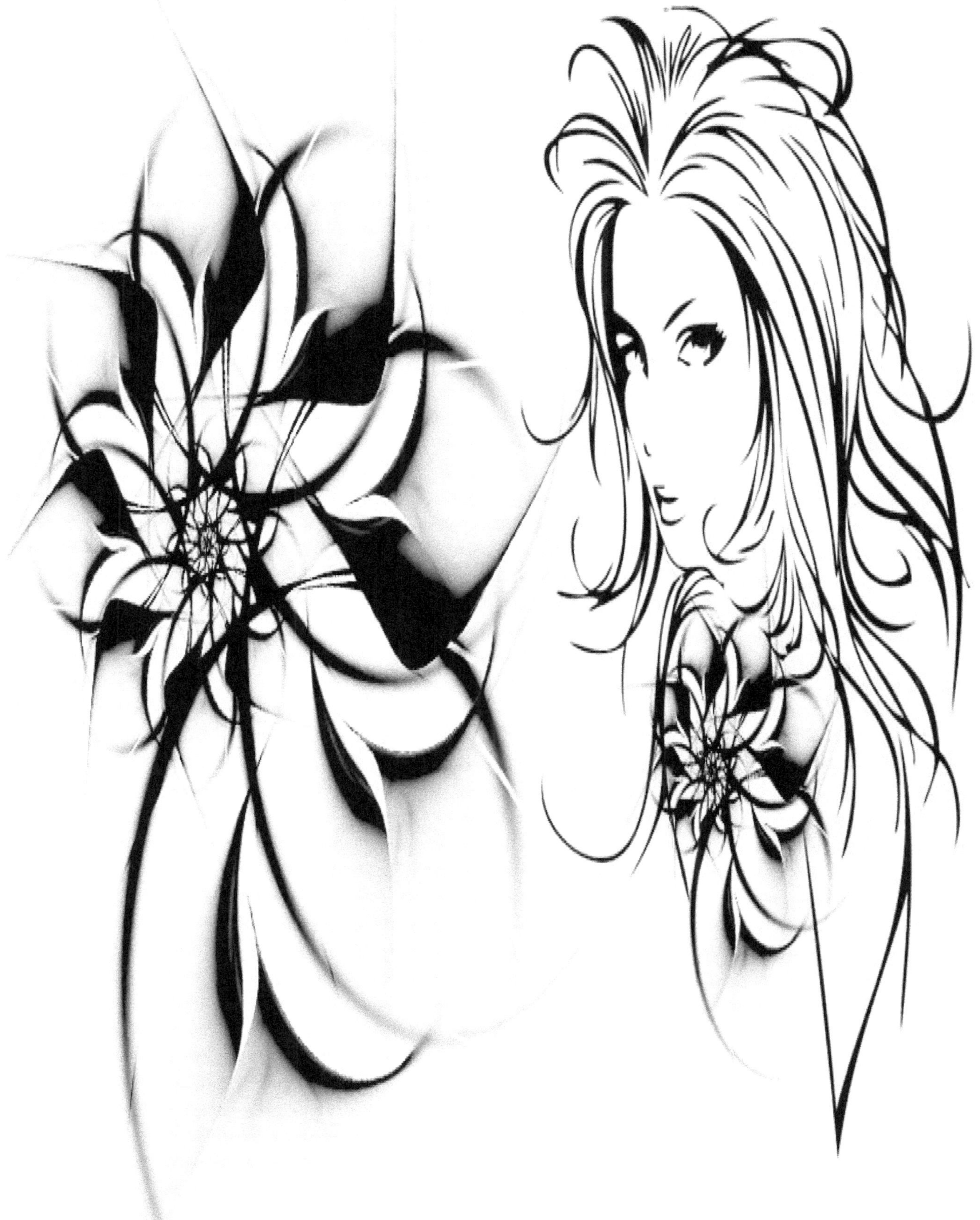

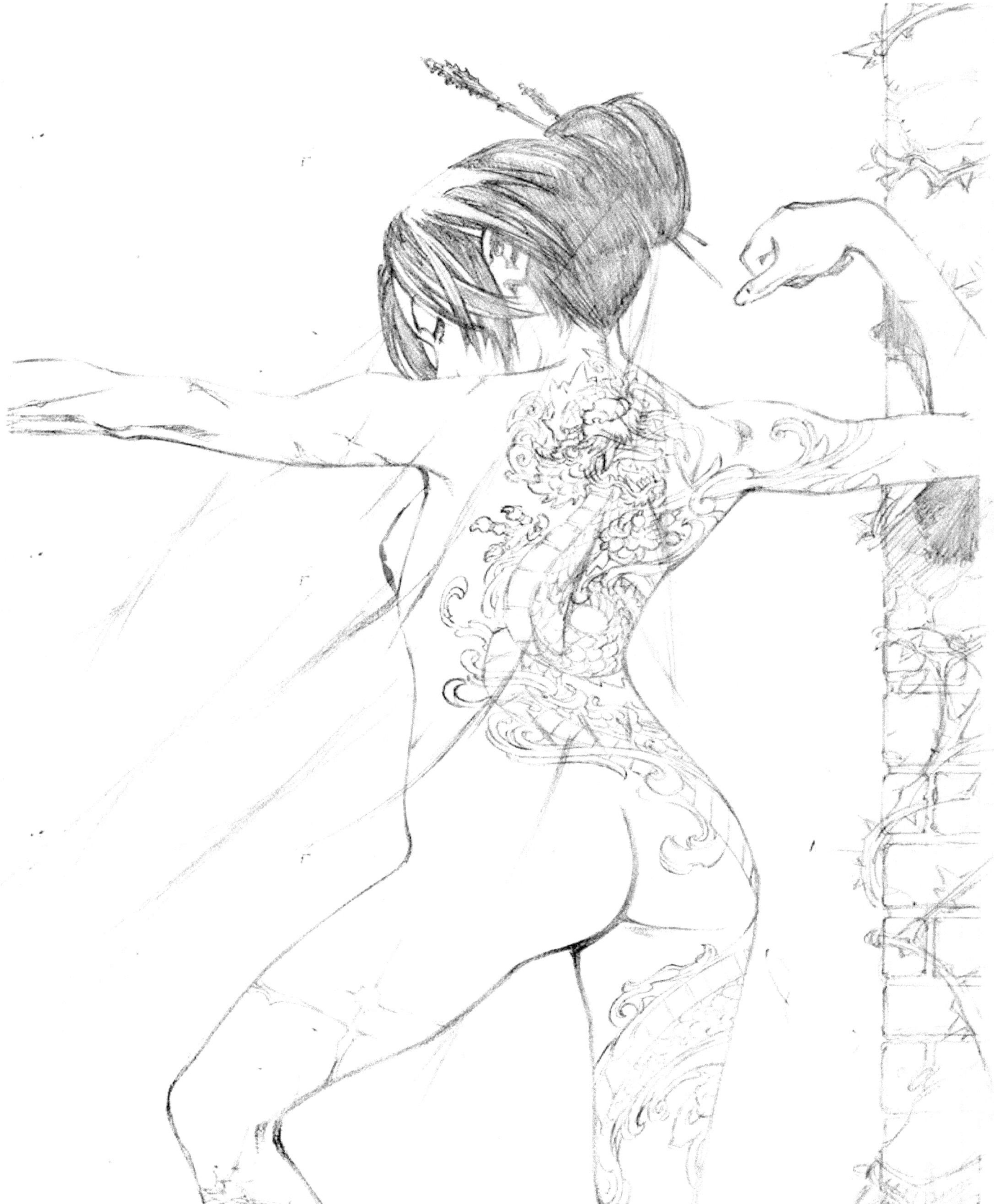

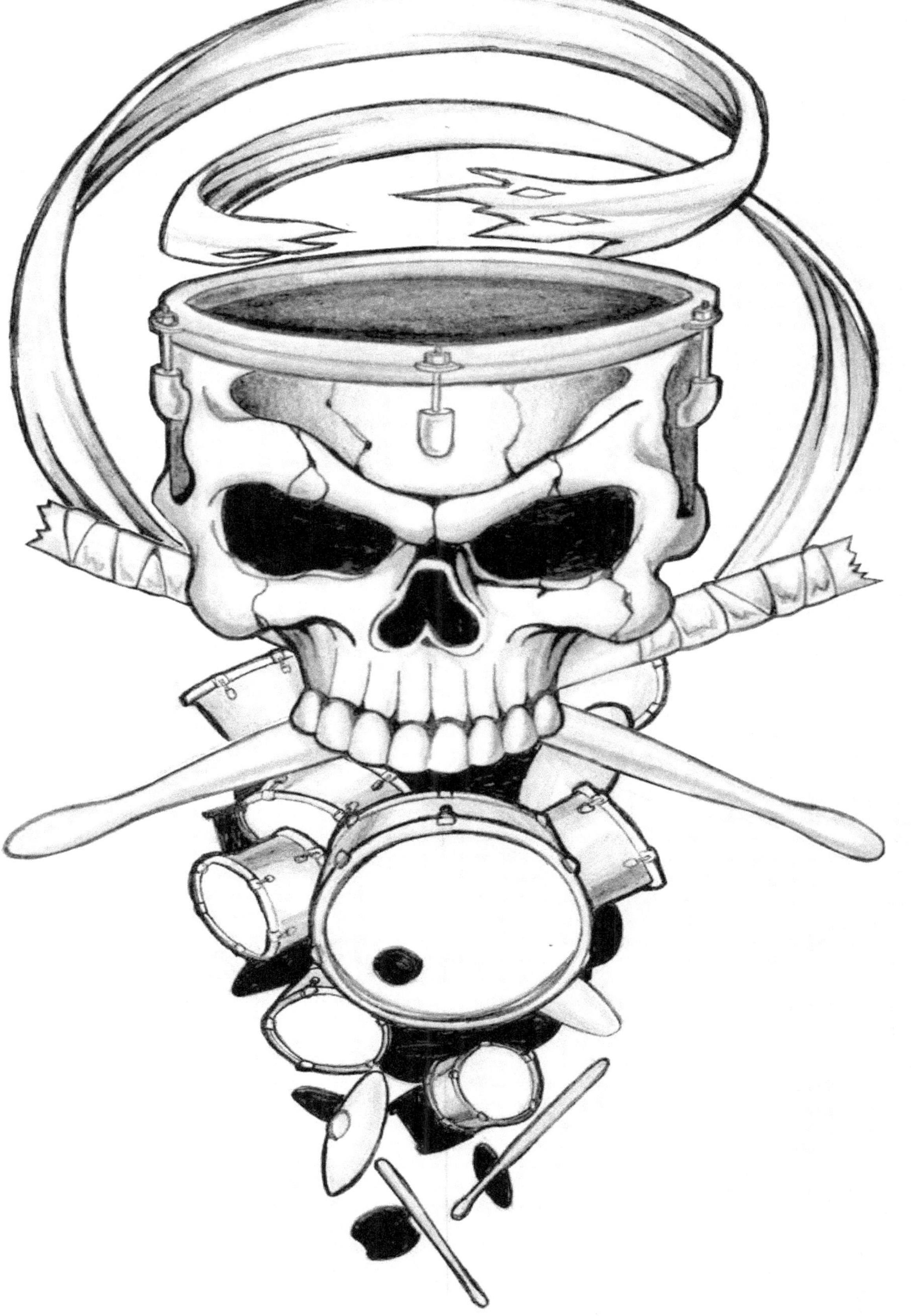

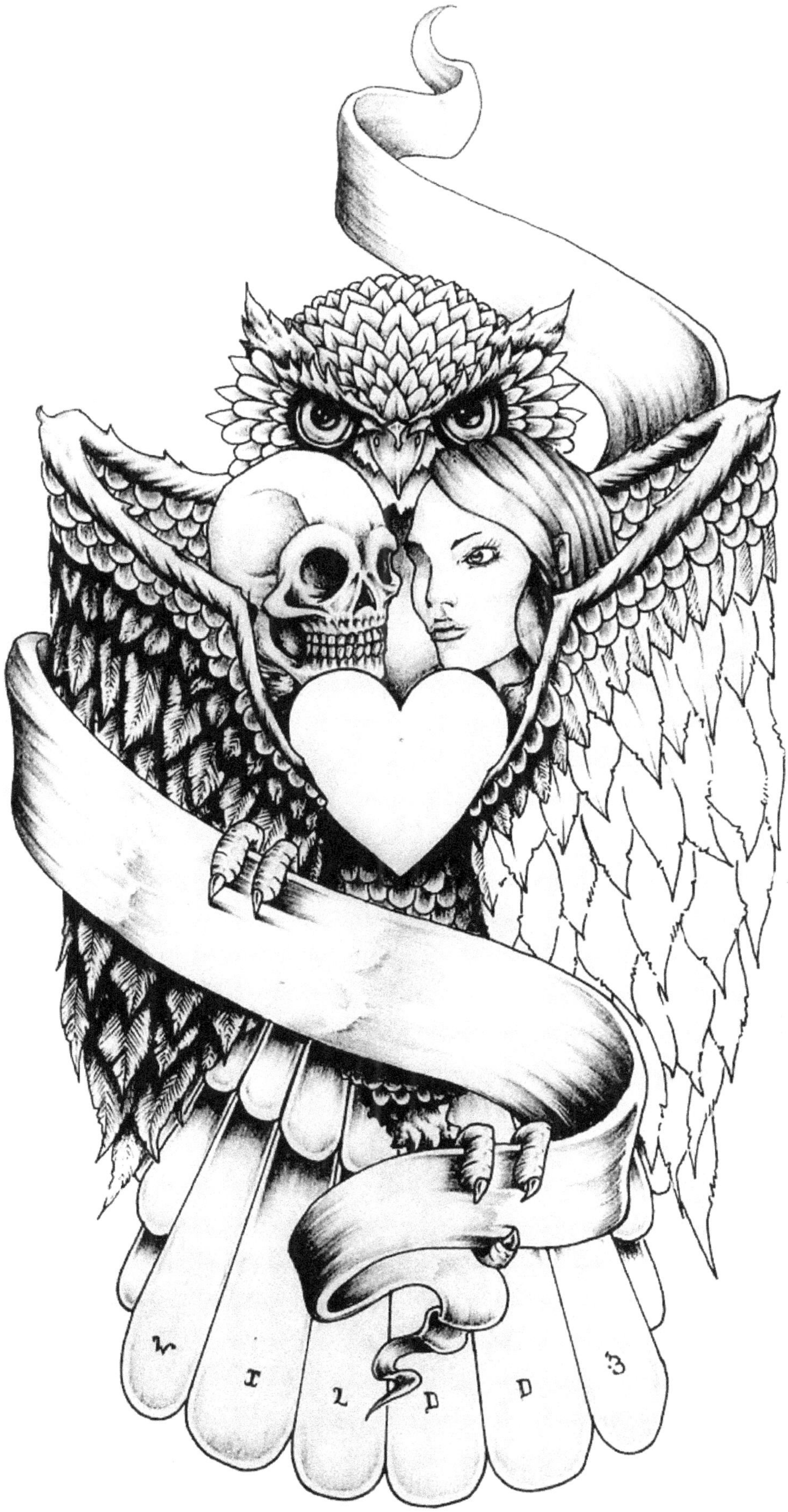

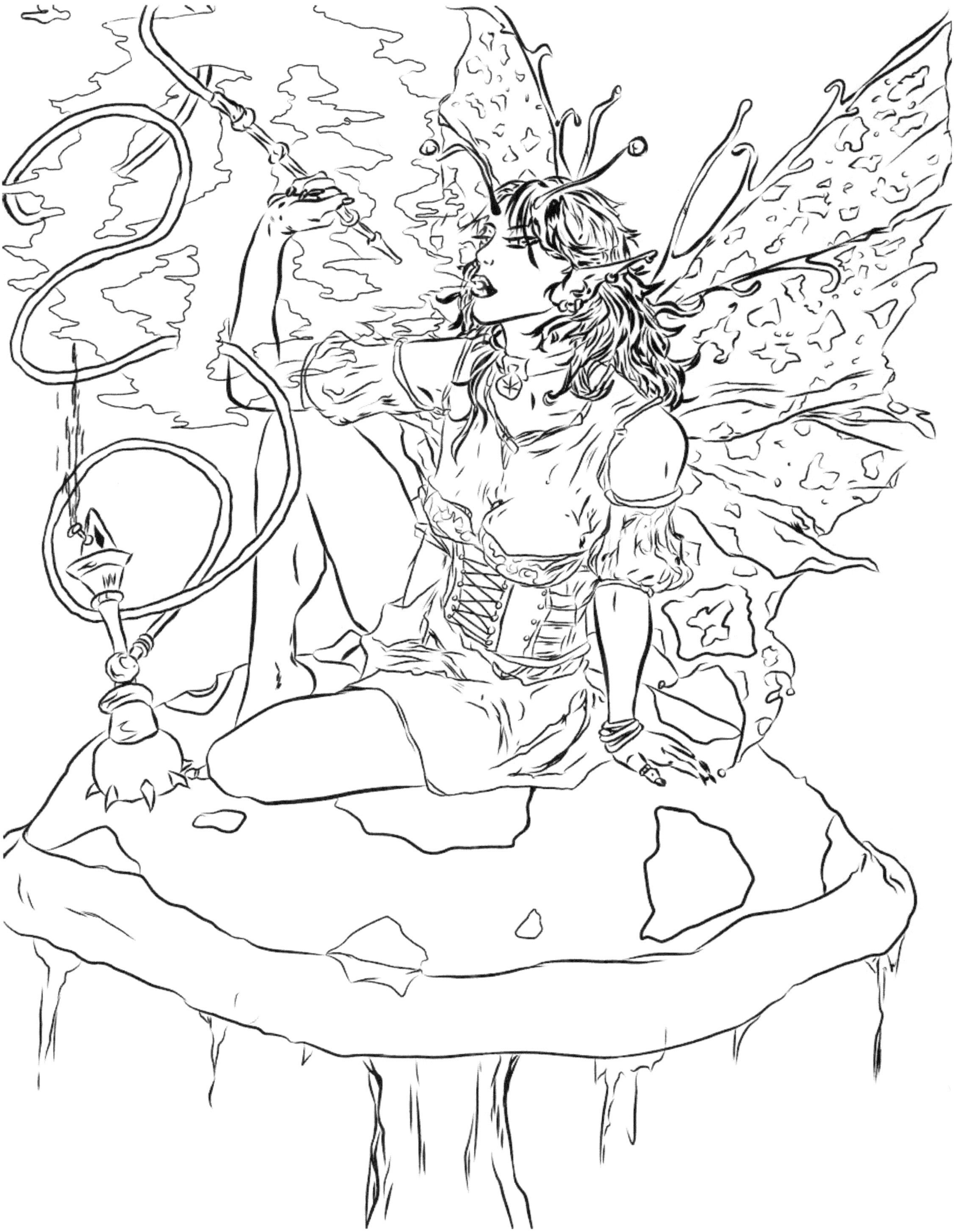

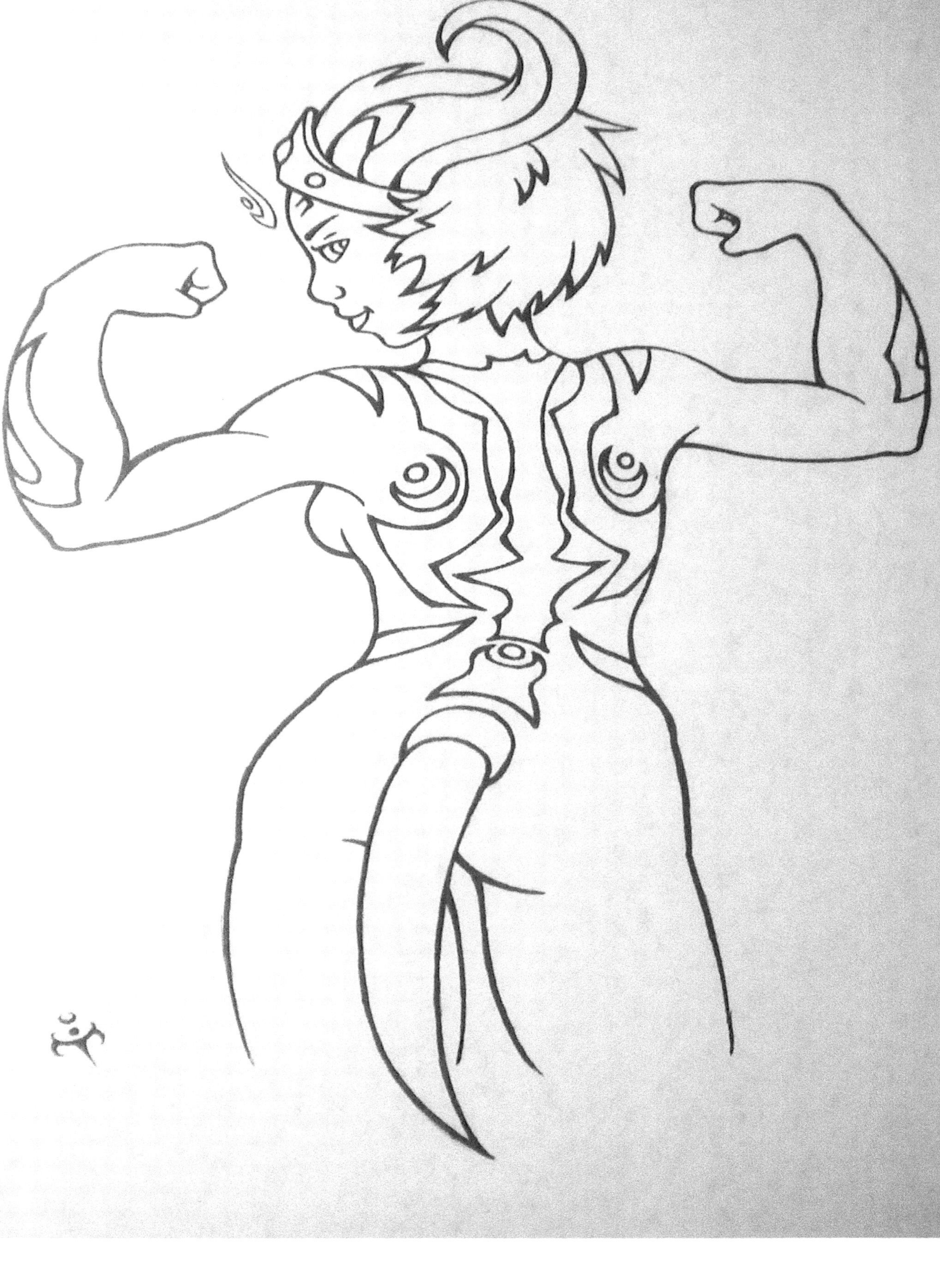

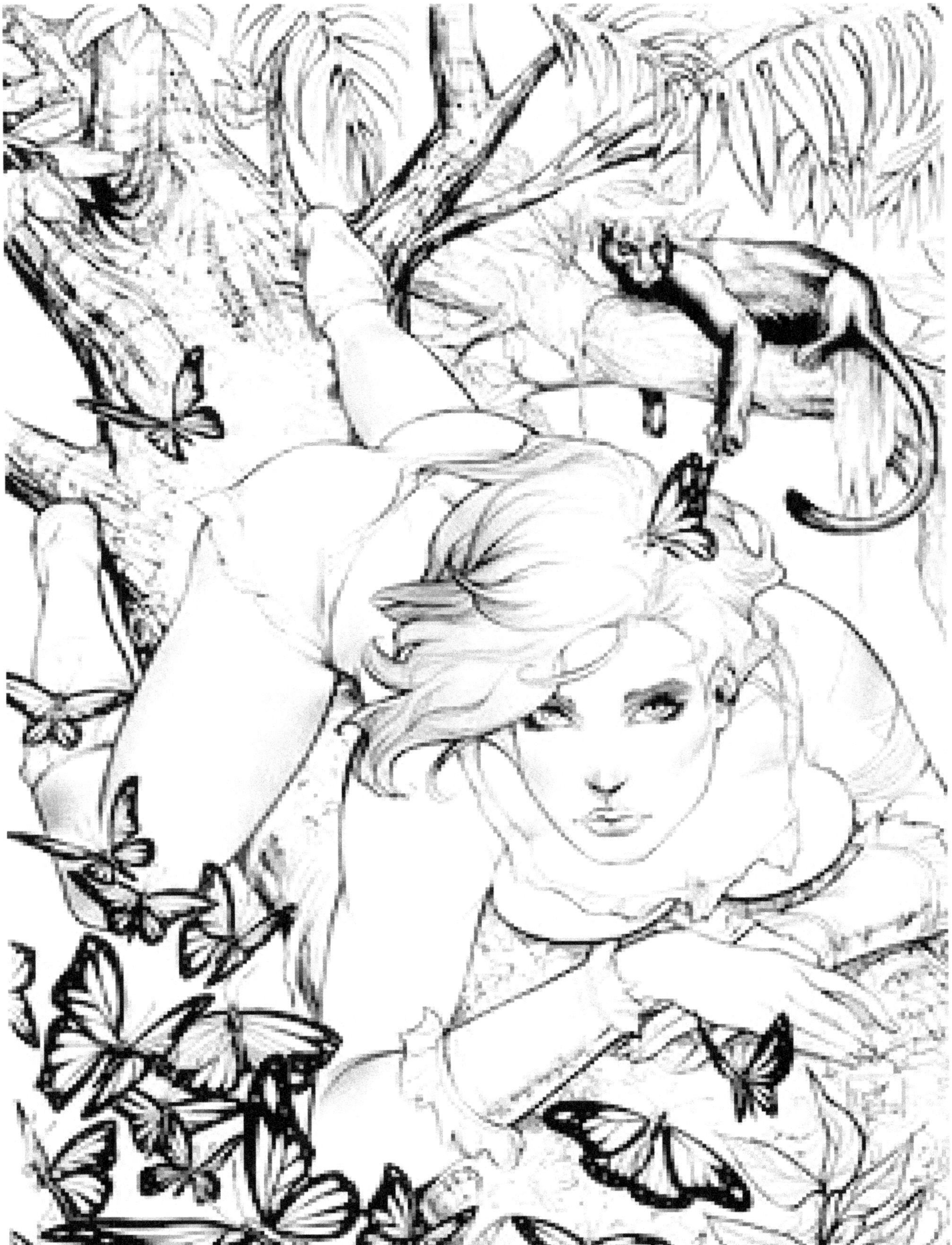

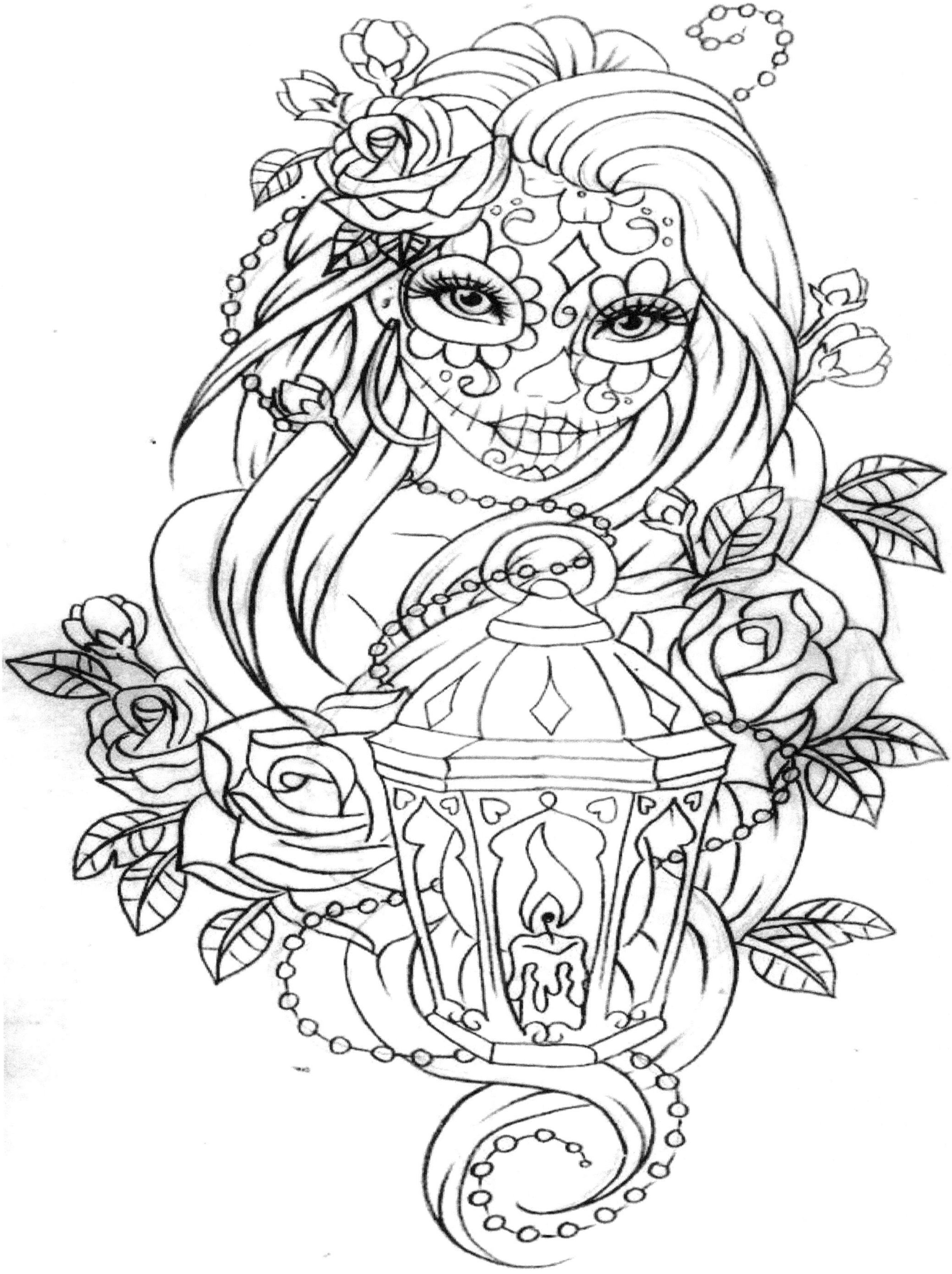

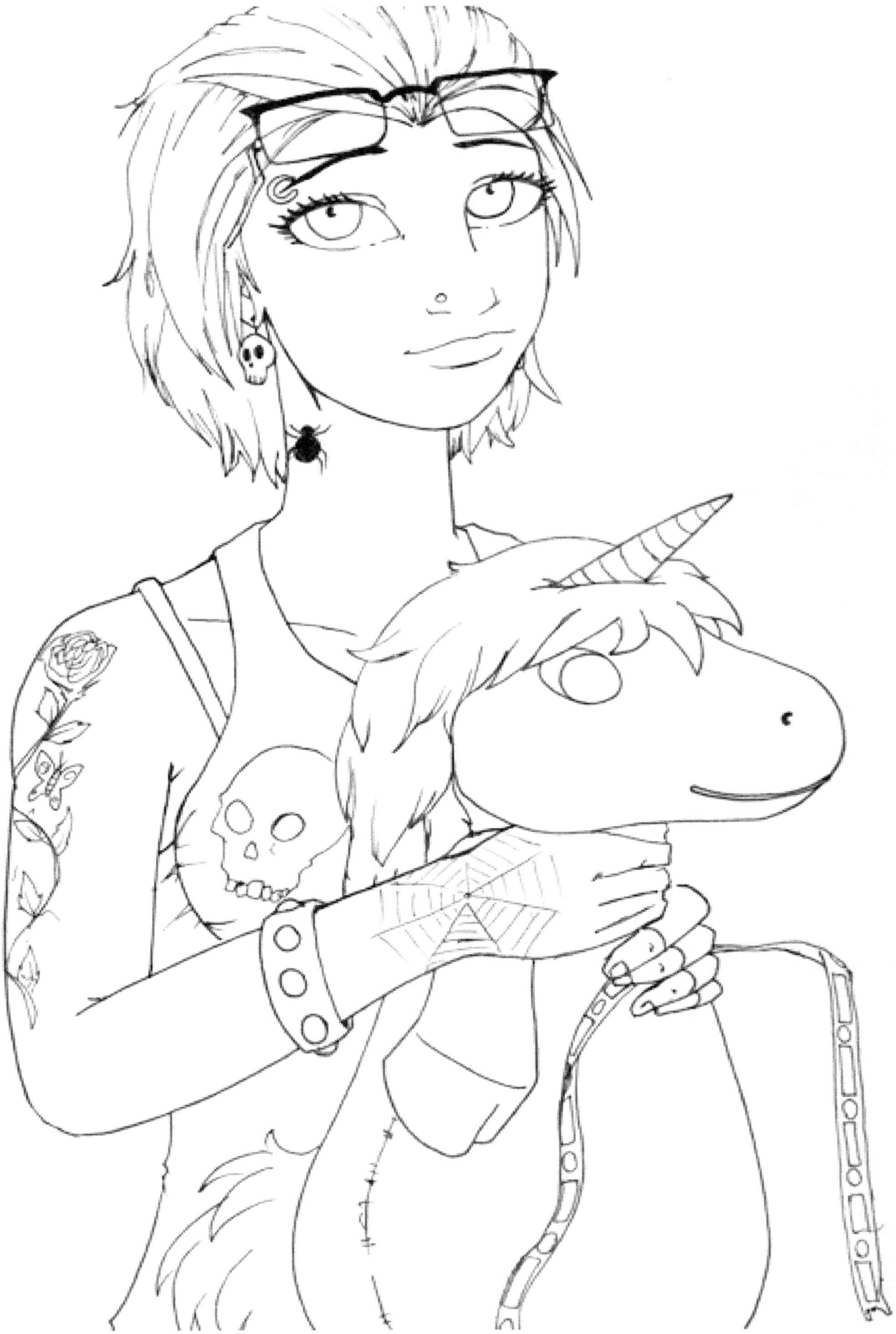

Love

FOREVER
LOVE

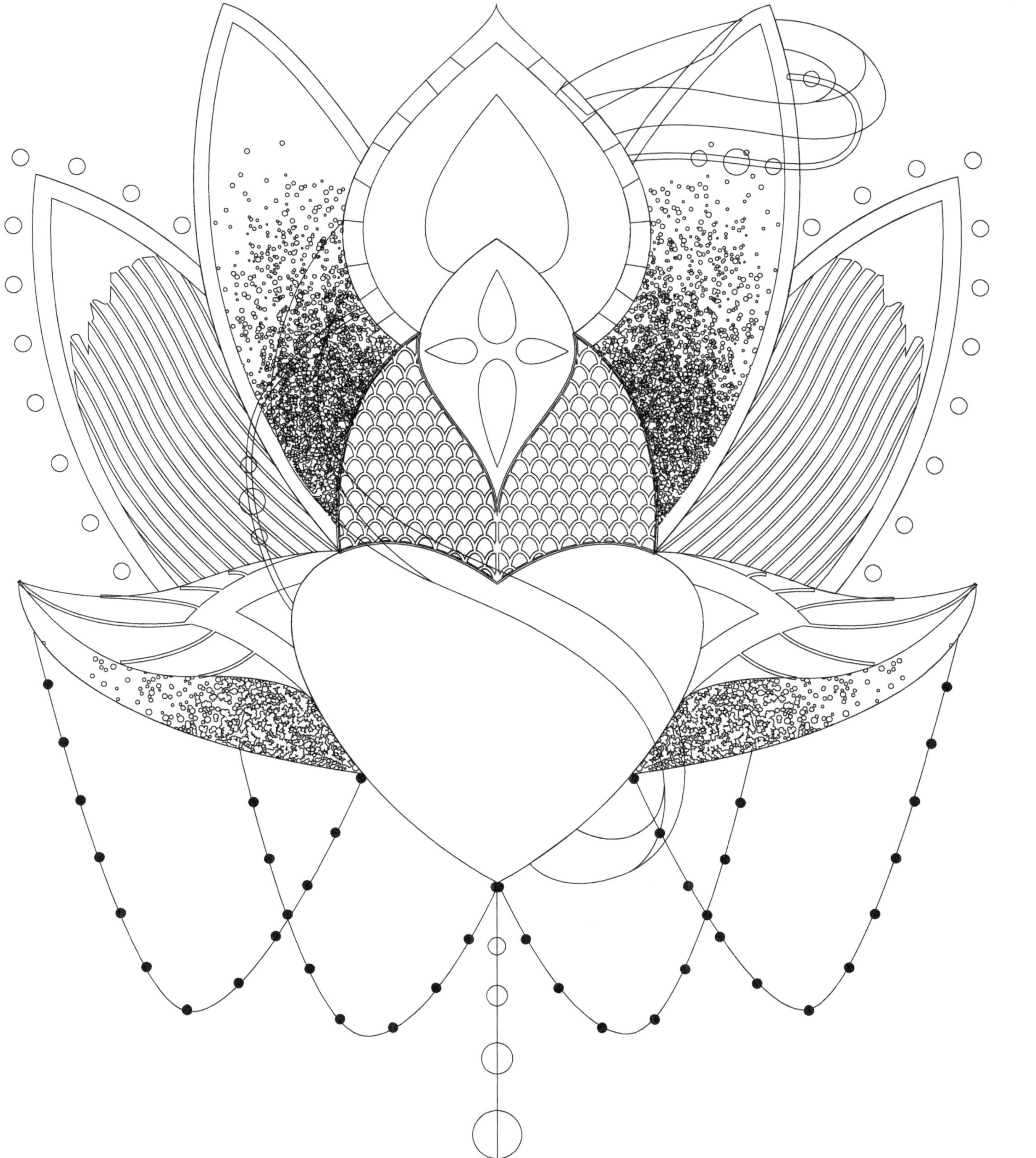

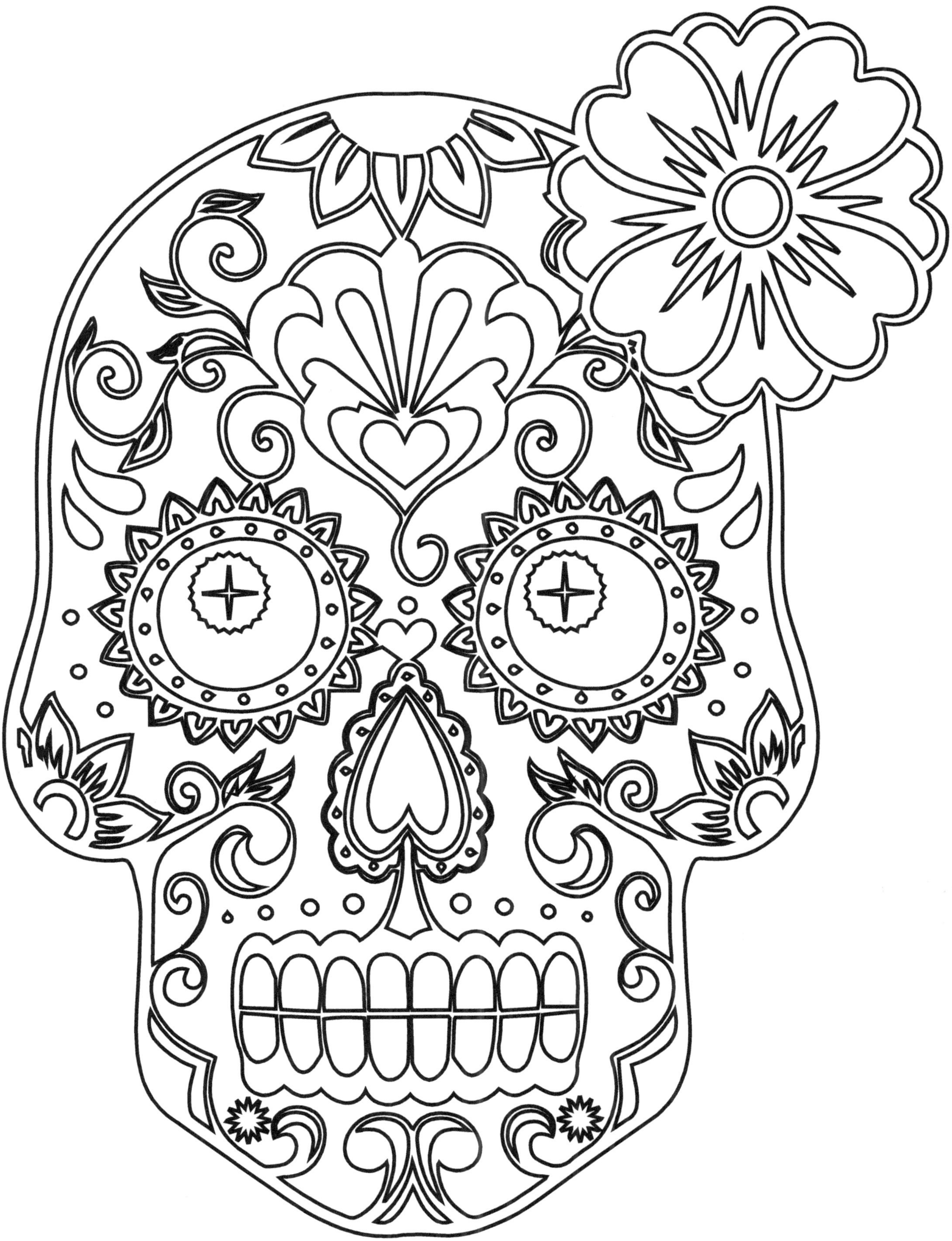

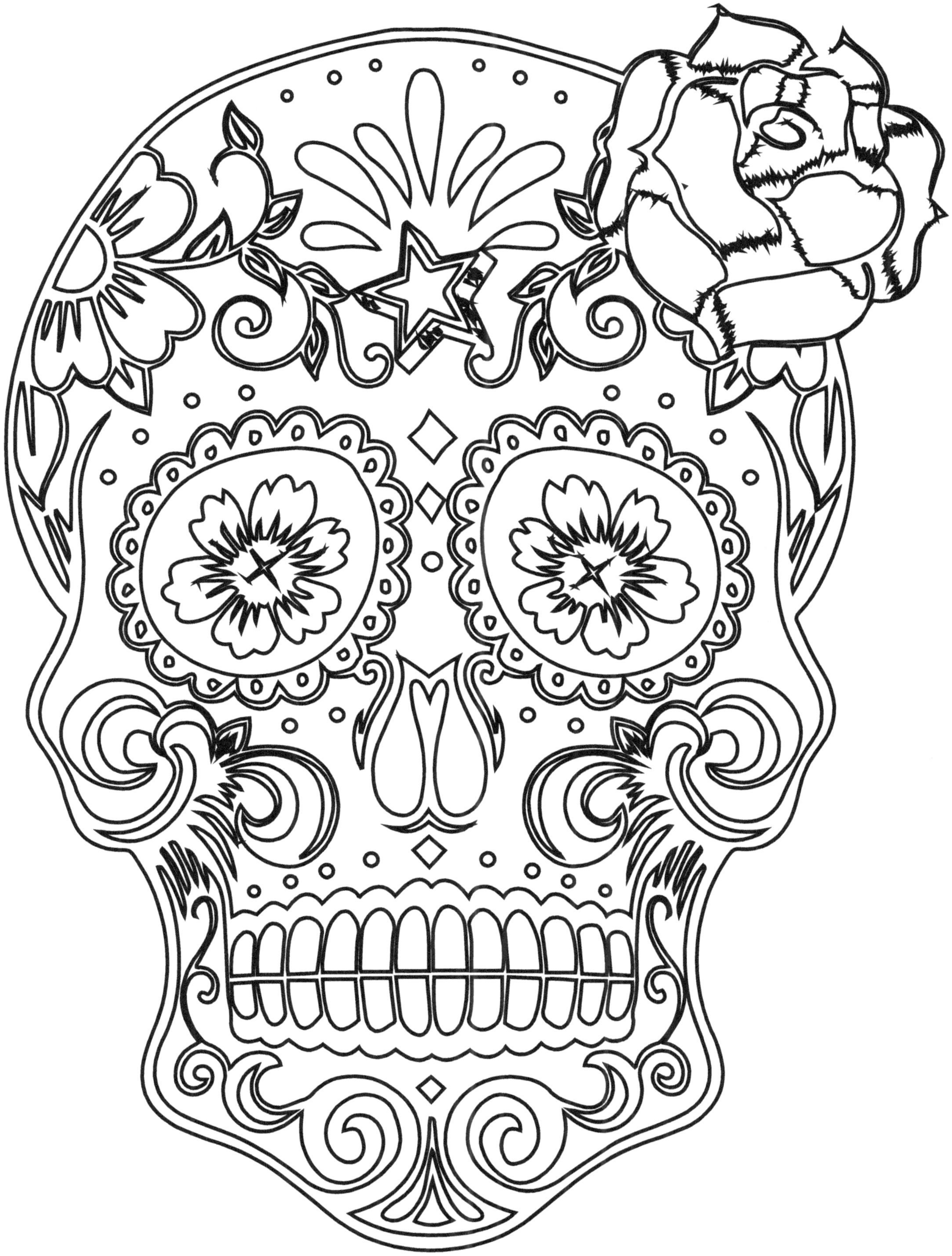

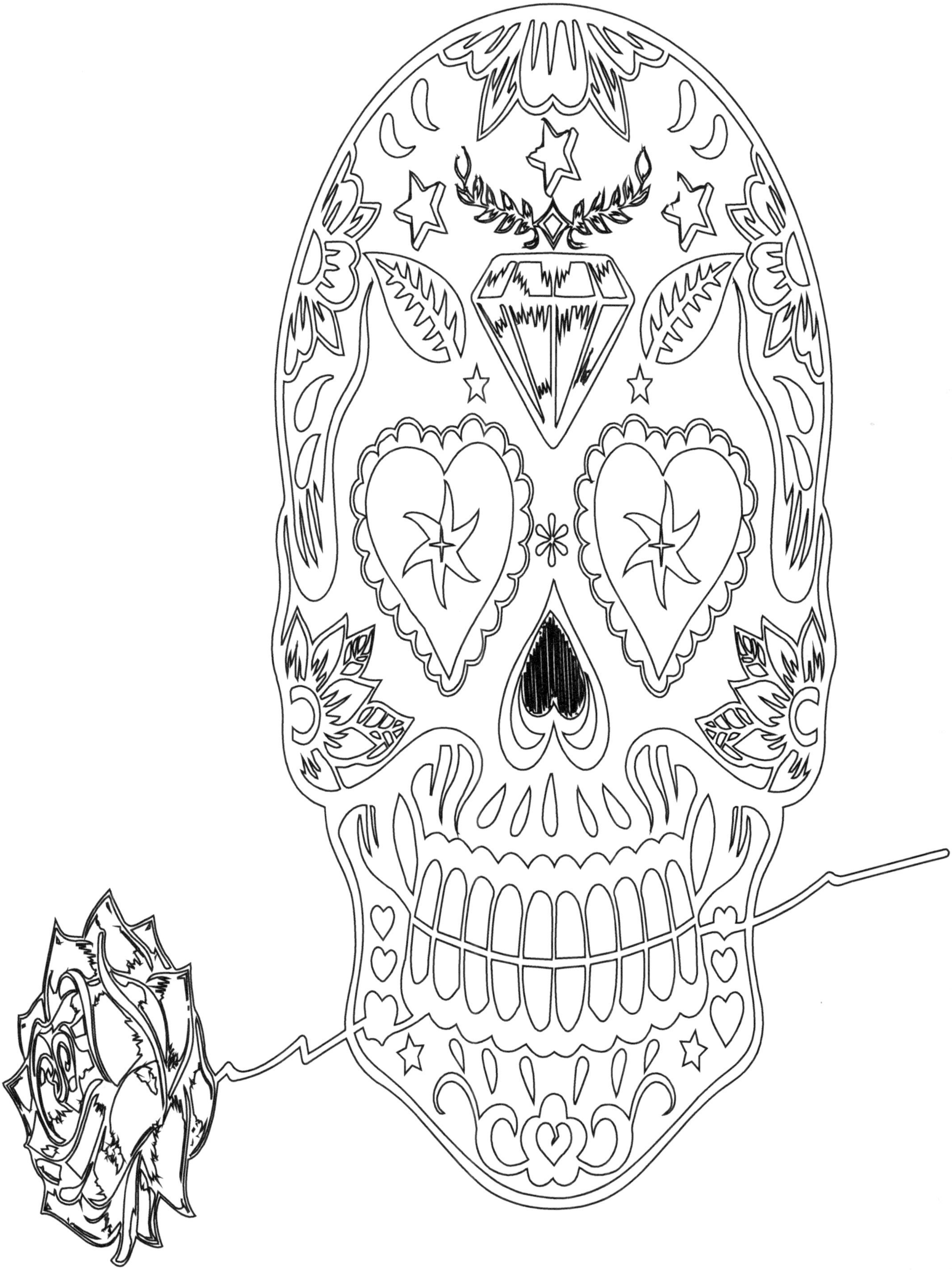

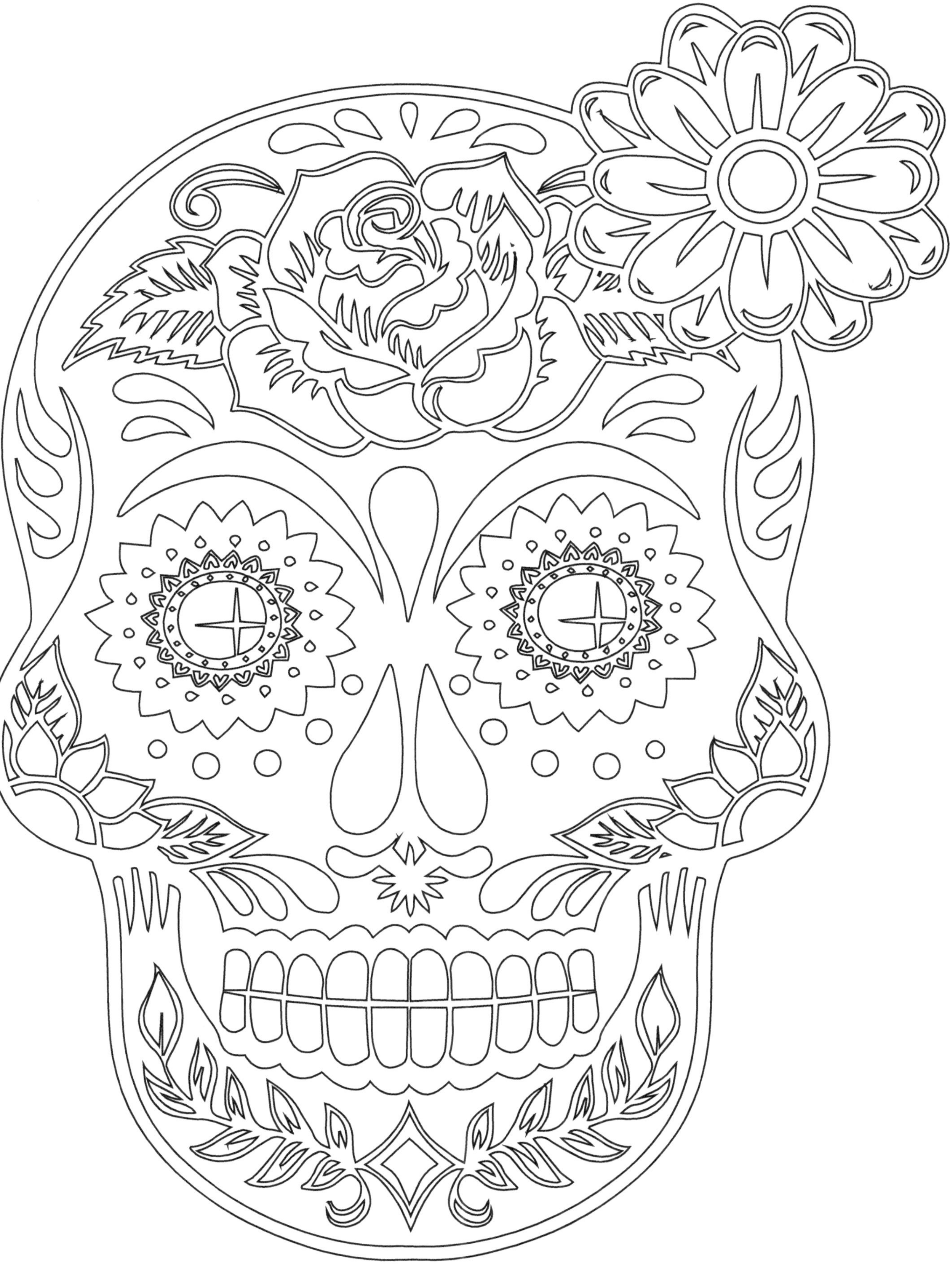

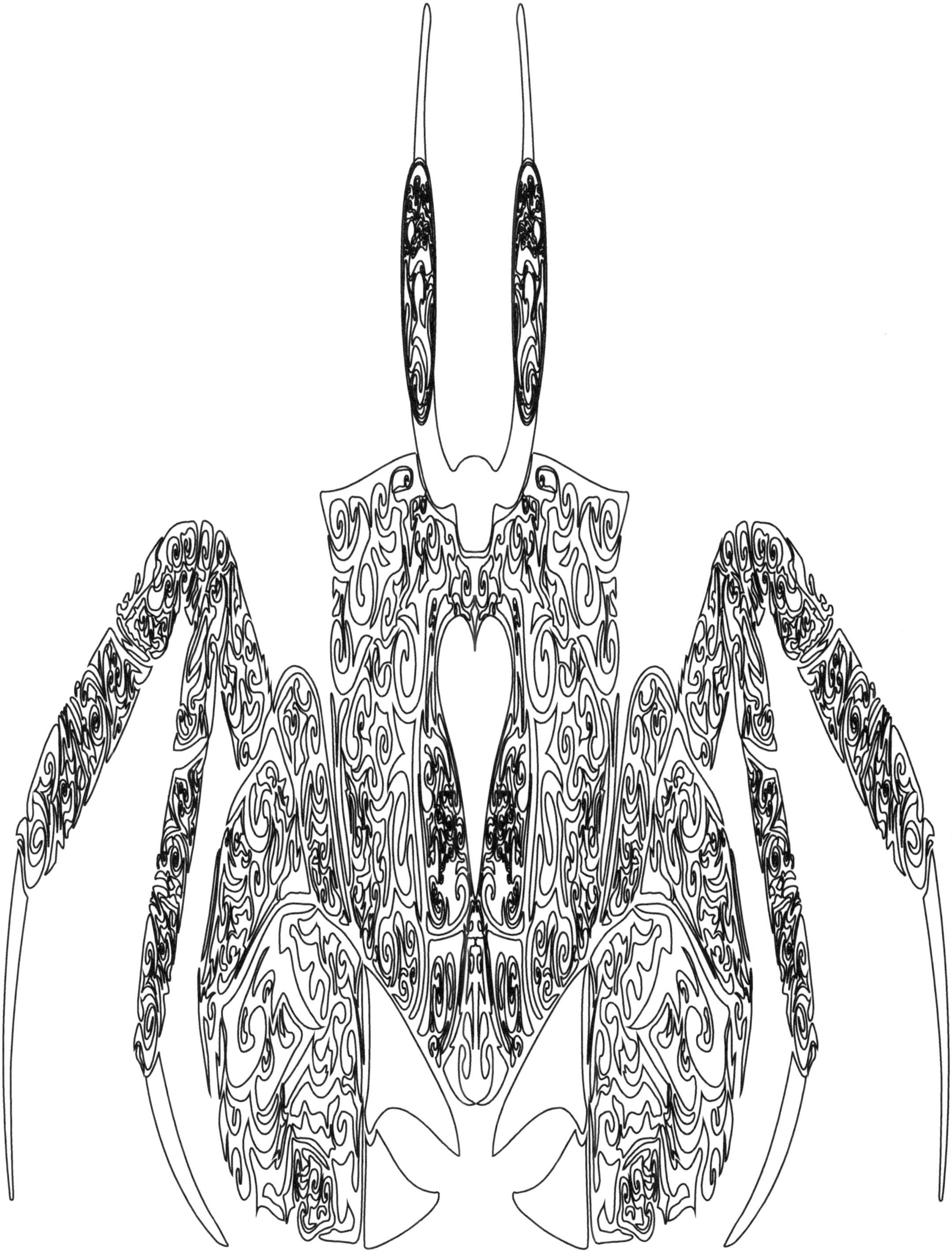

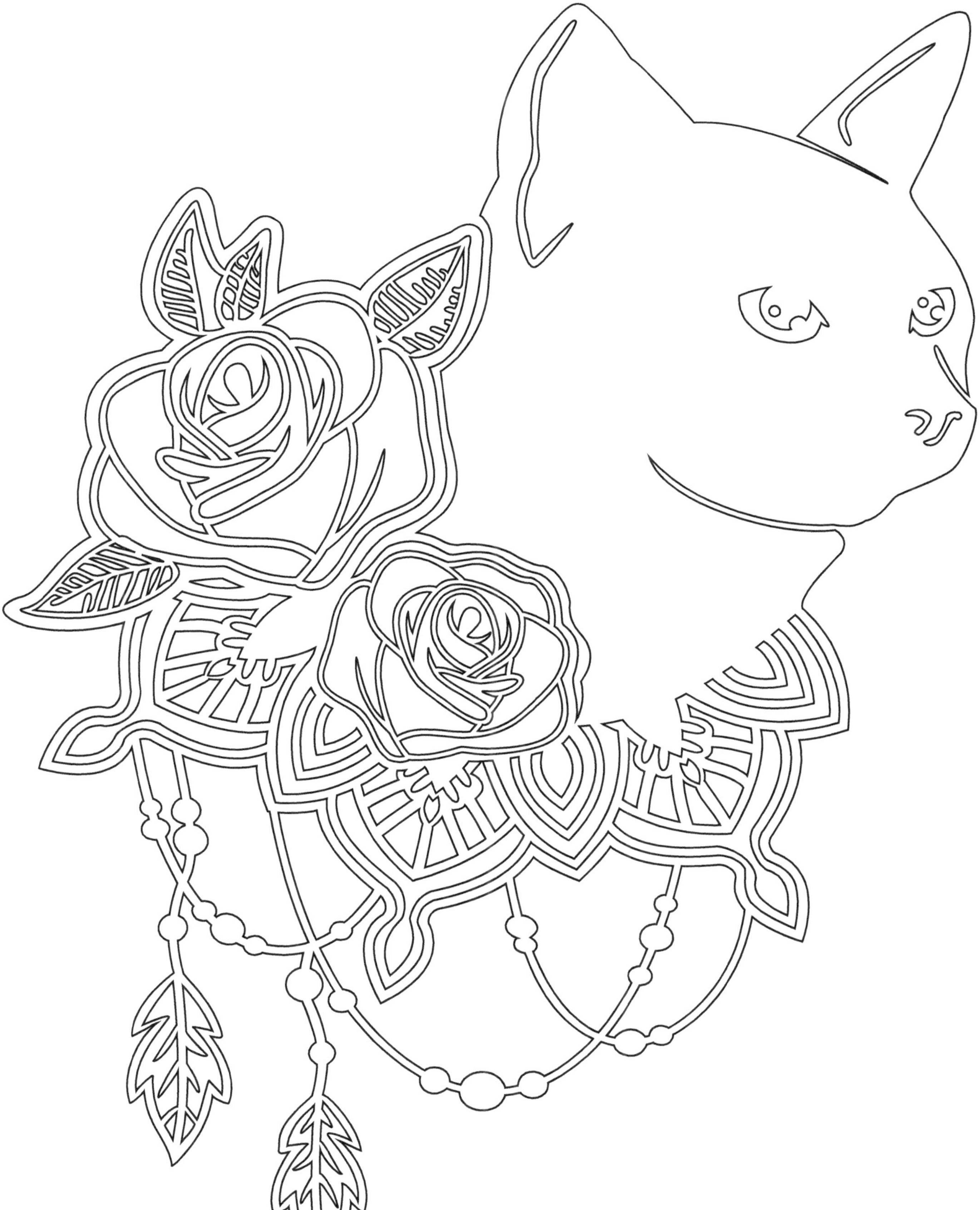

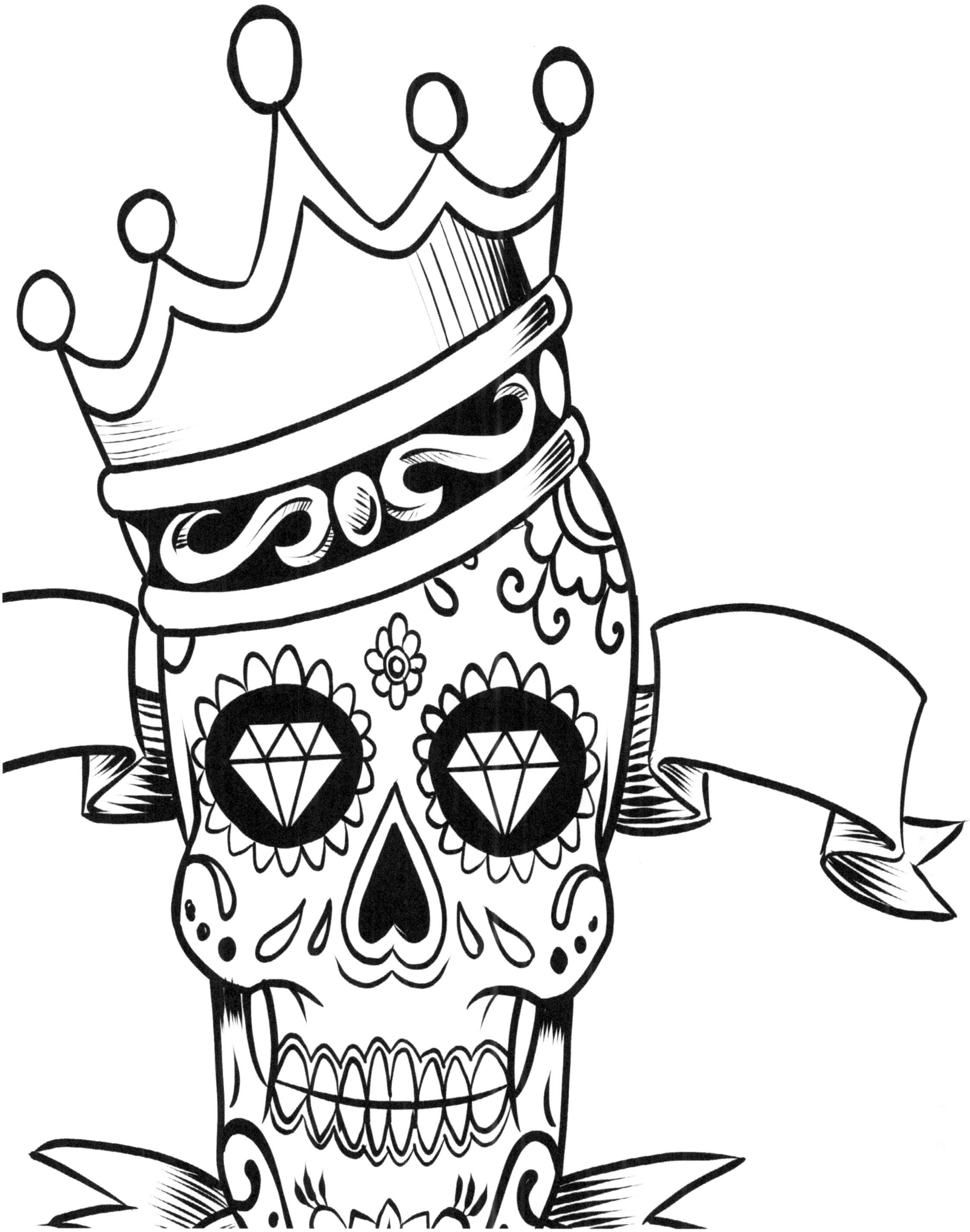

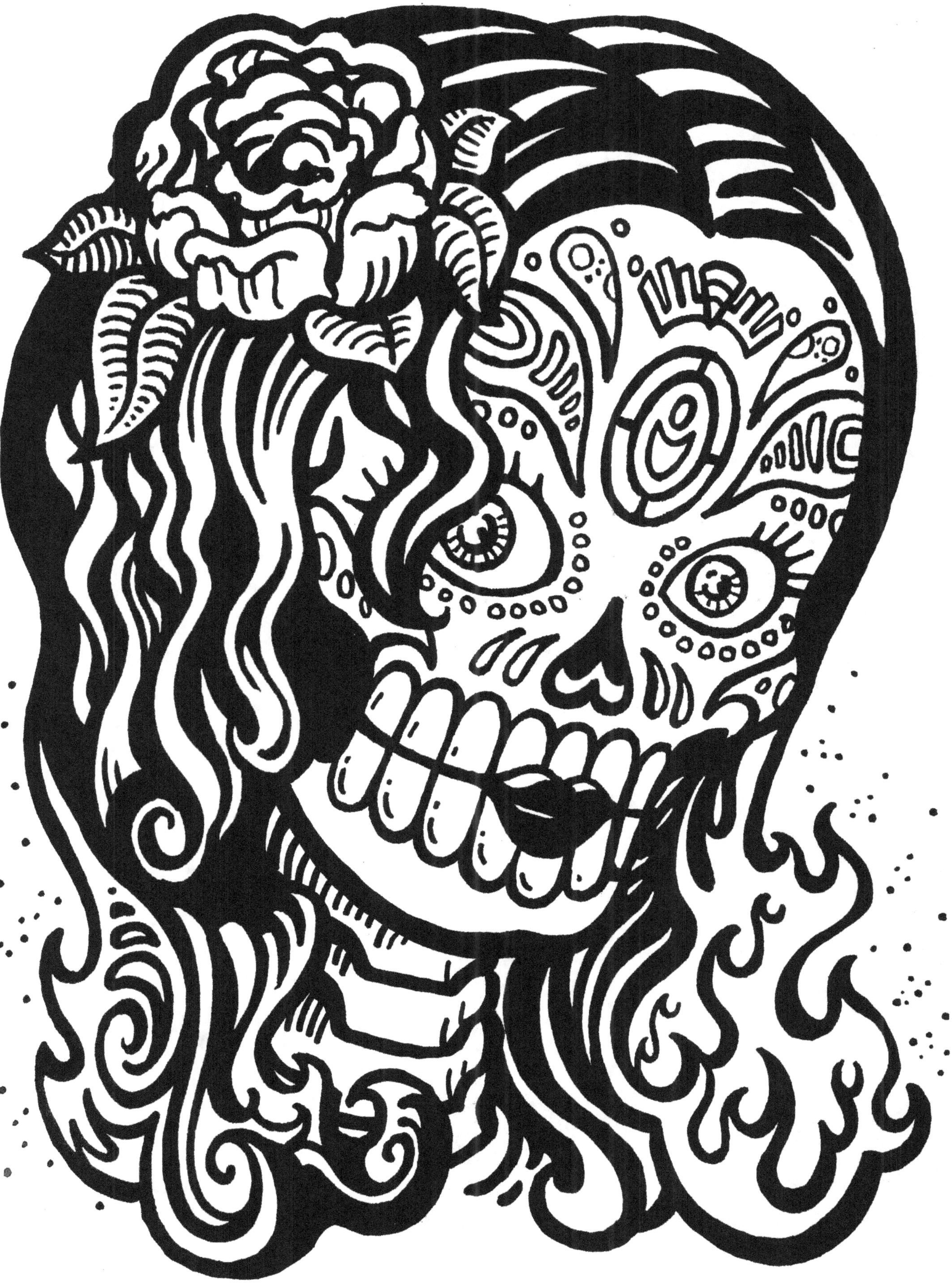

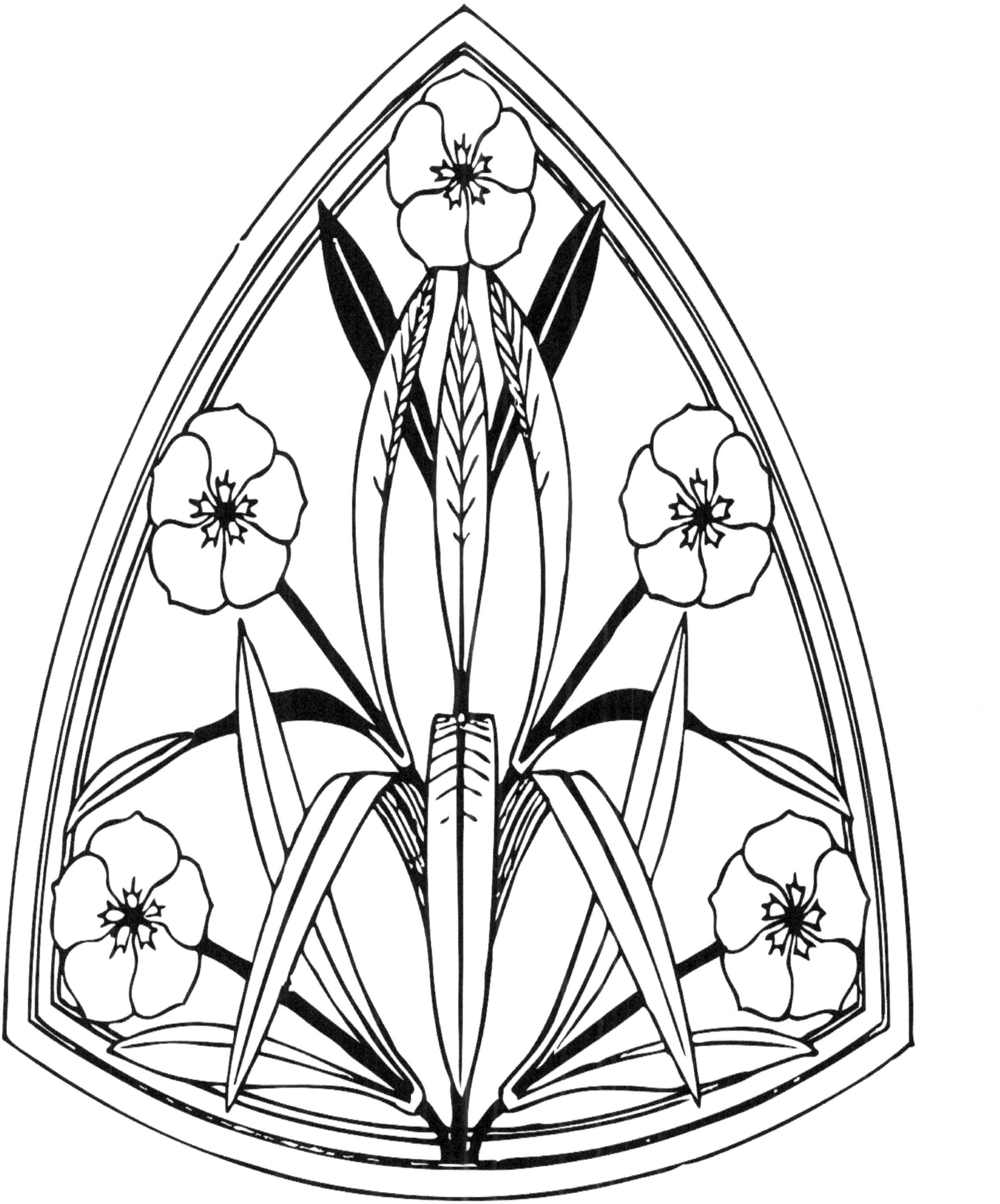

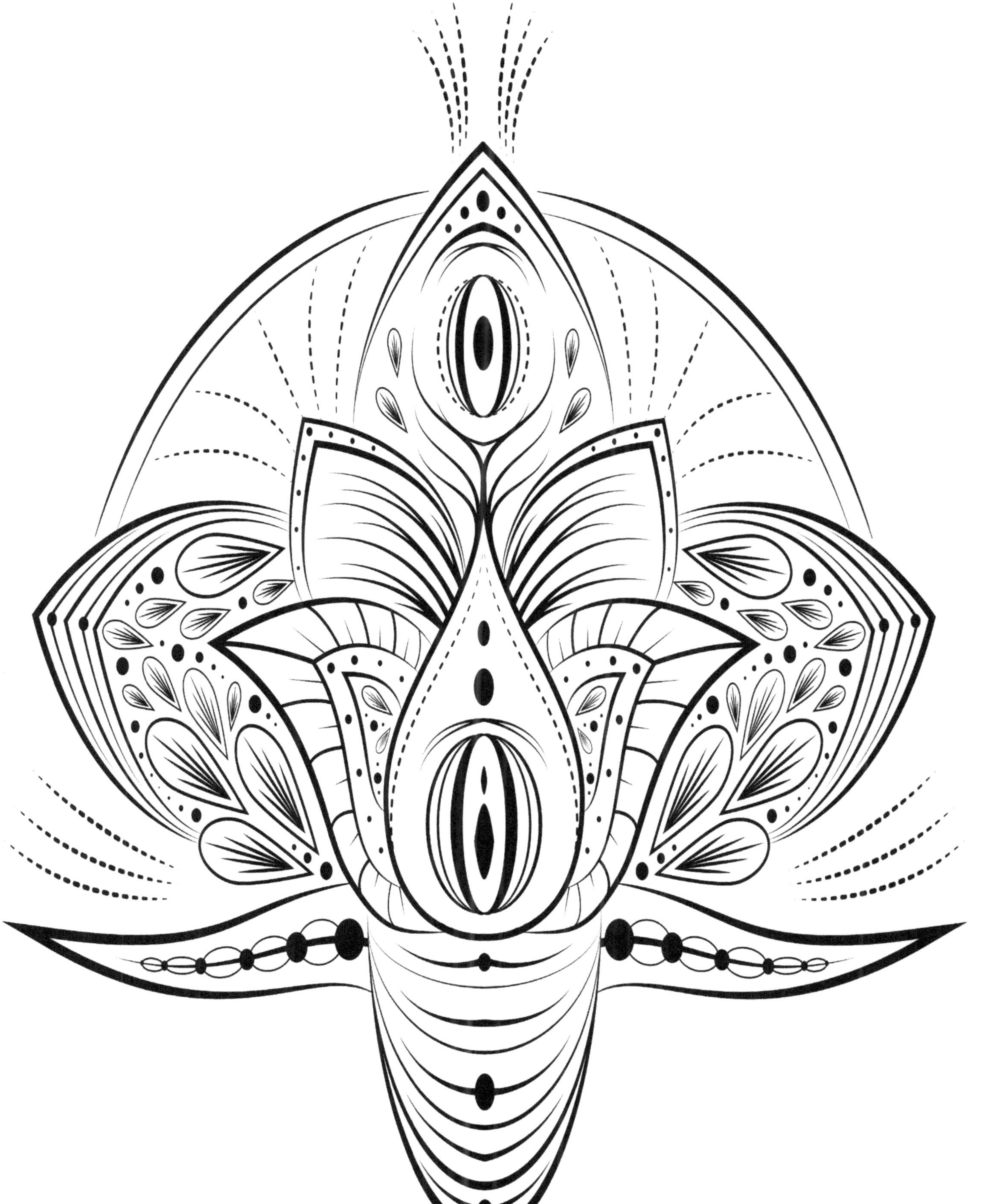

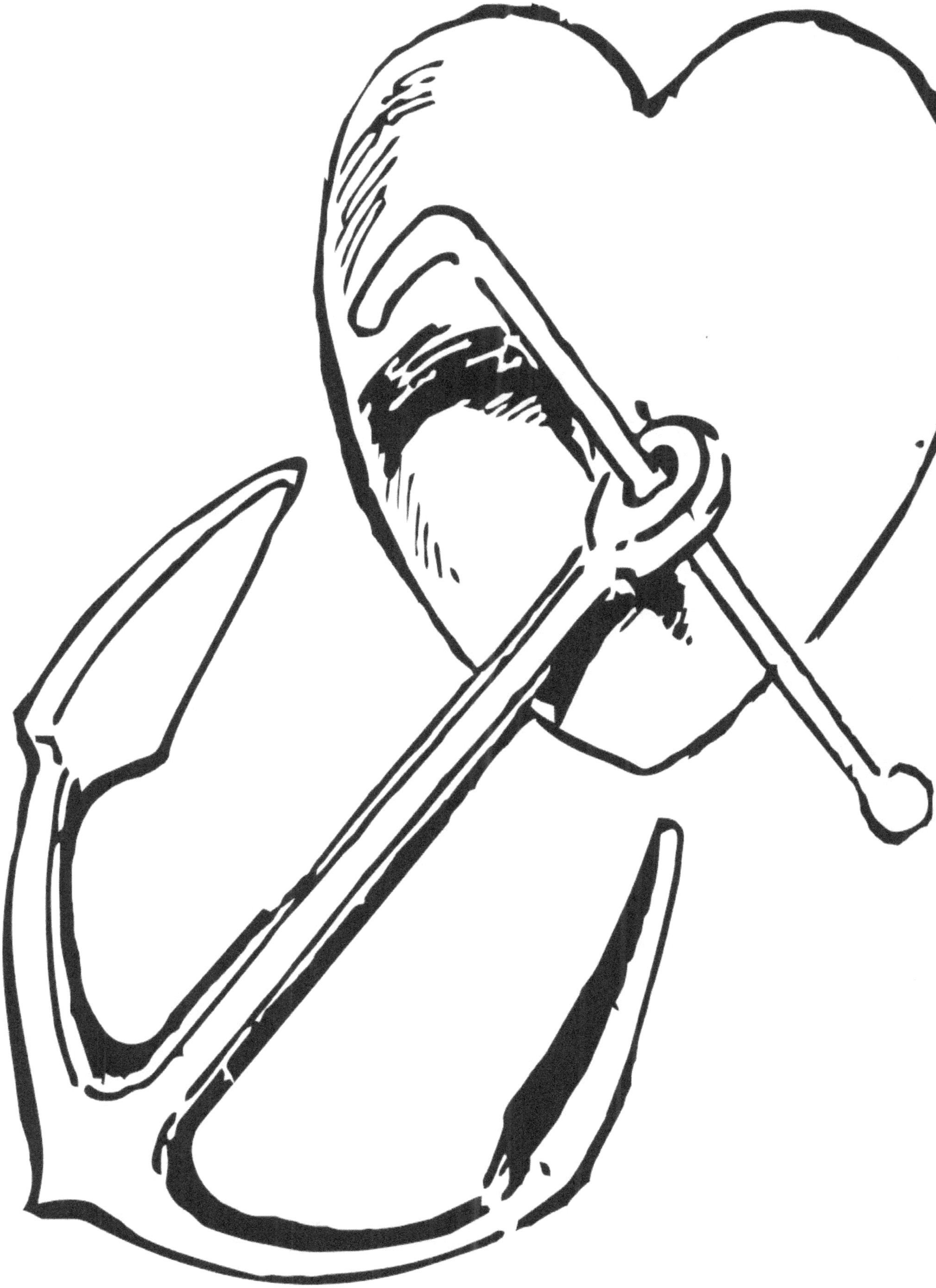

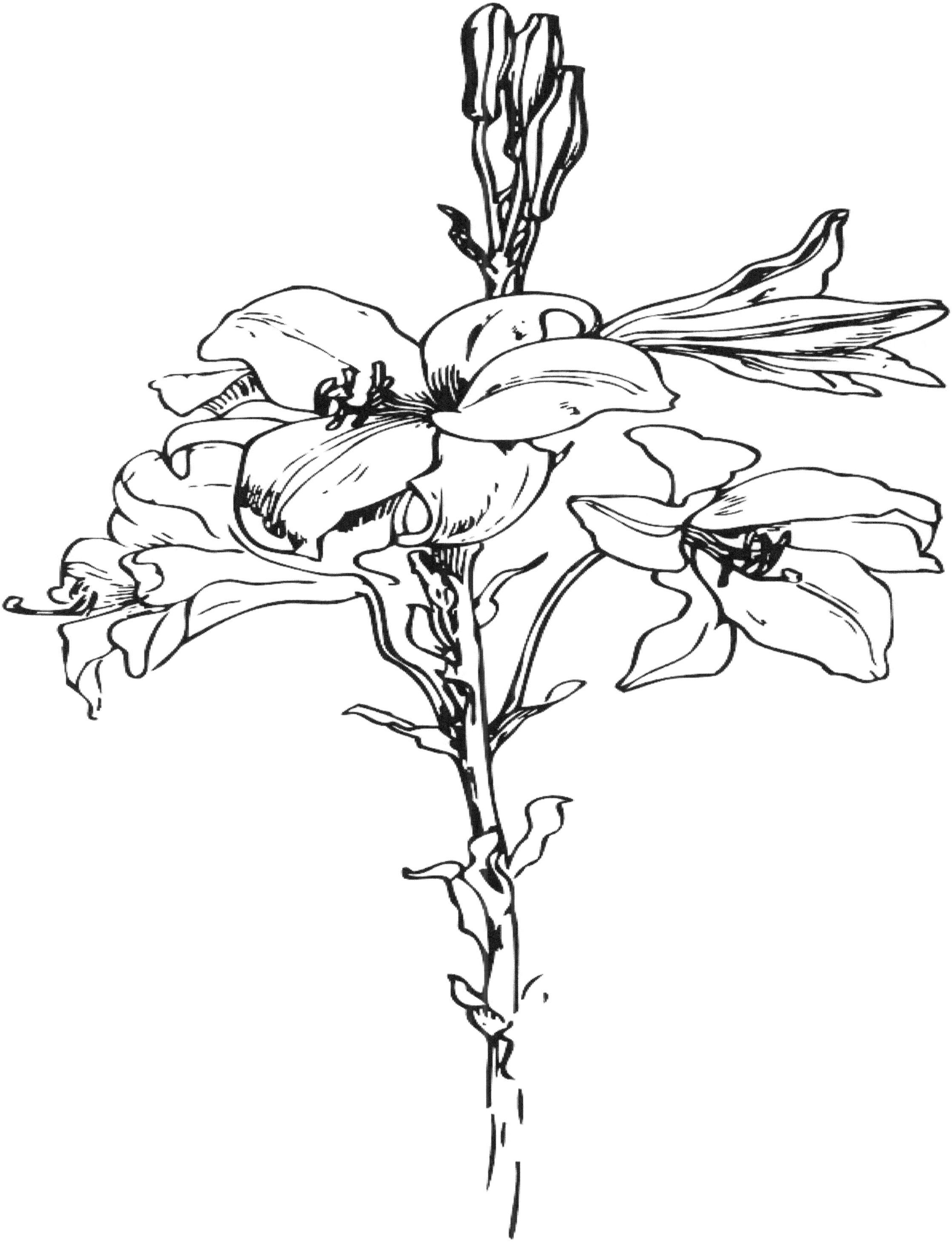

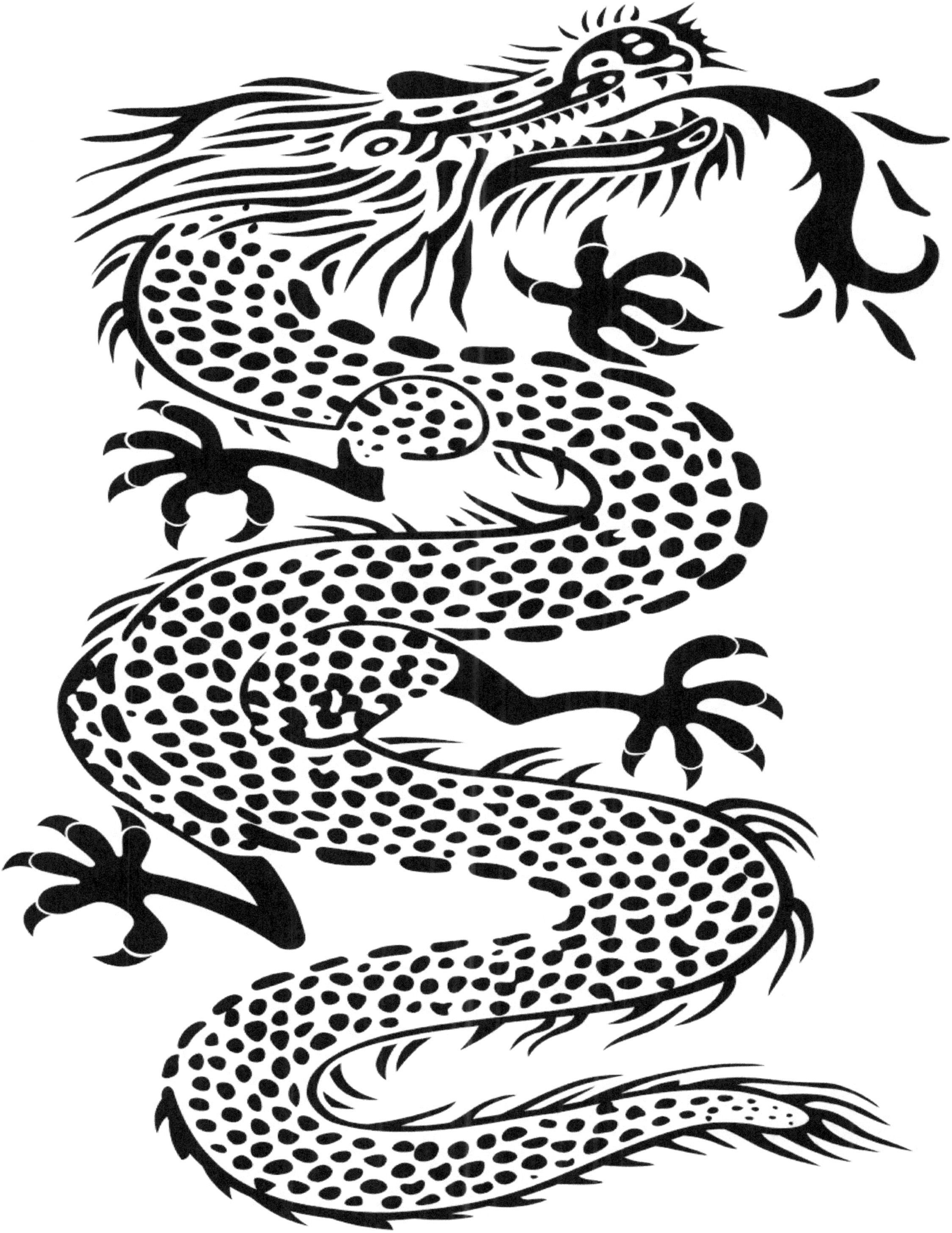

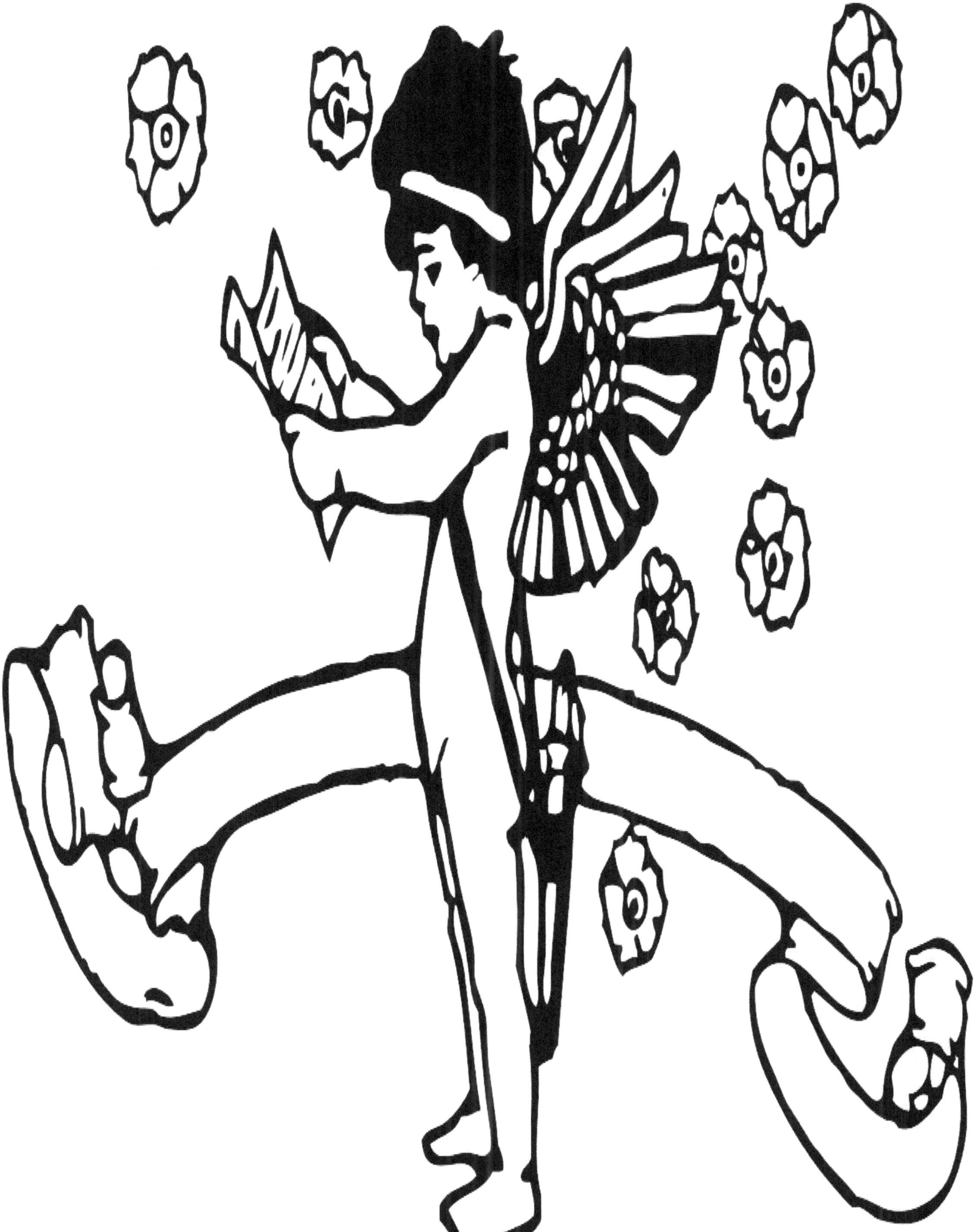

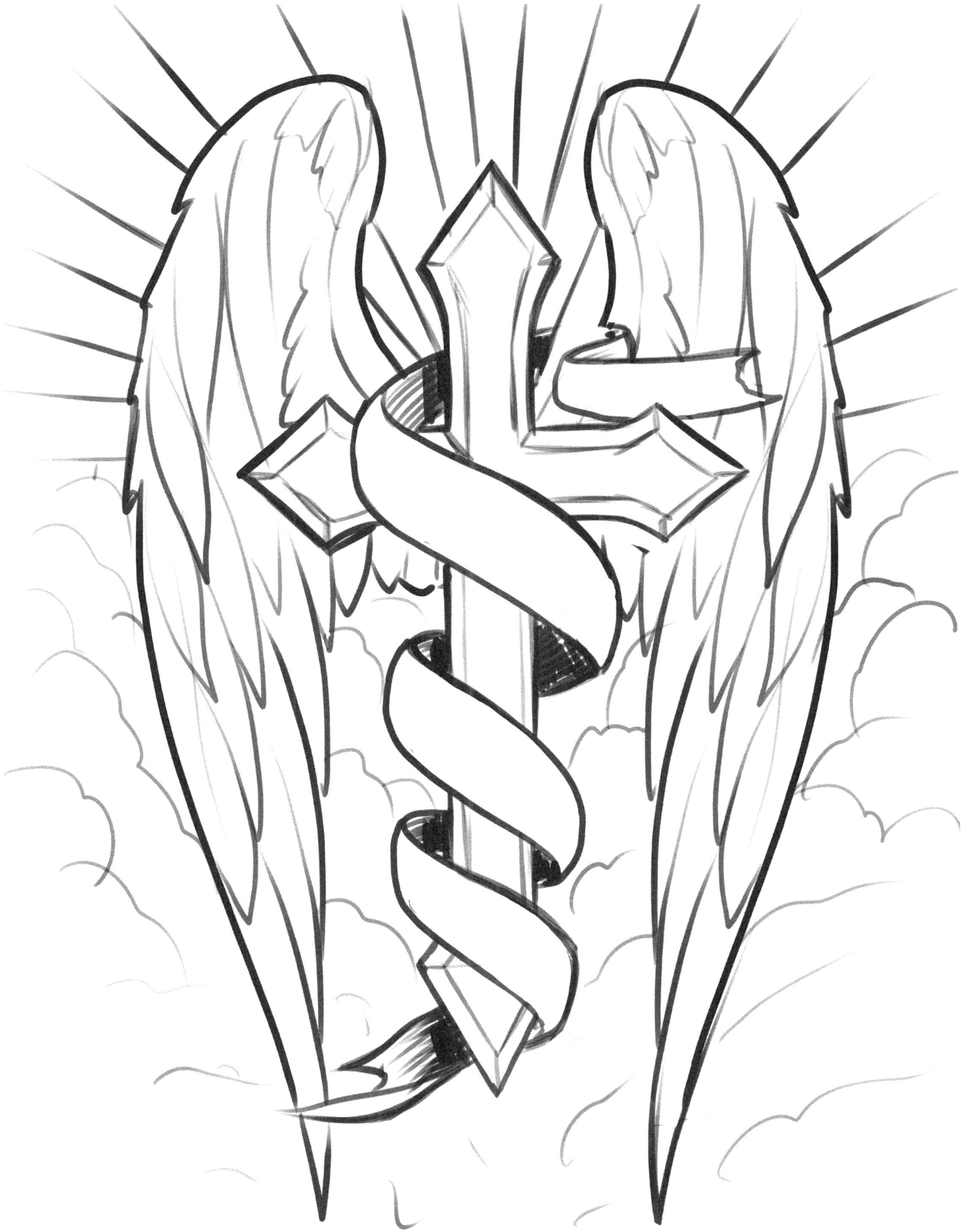

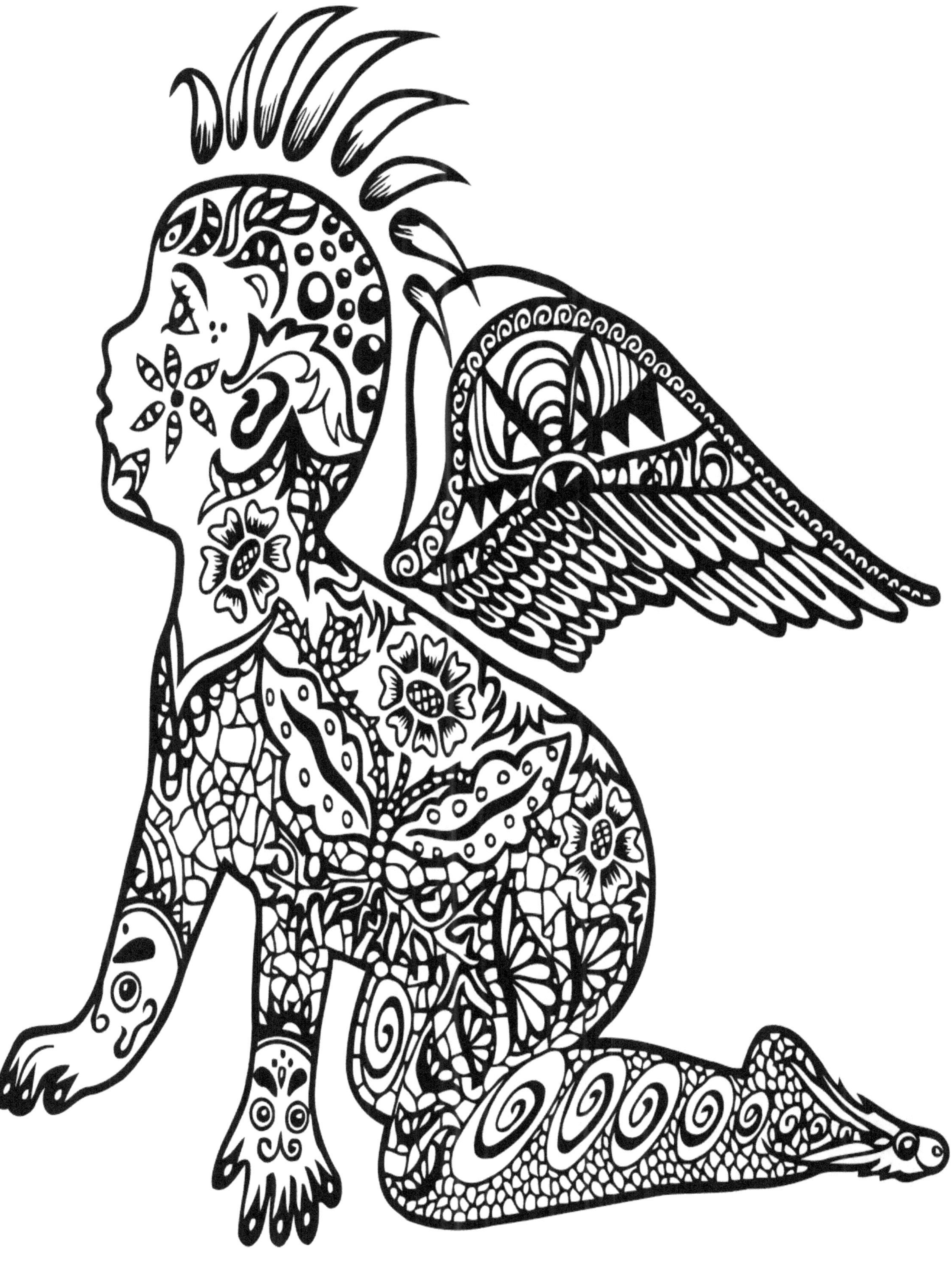

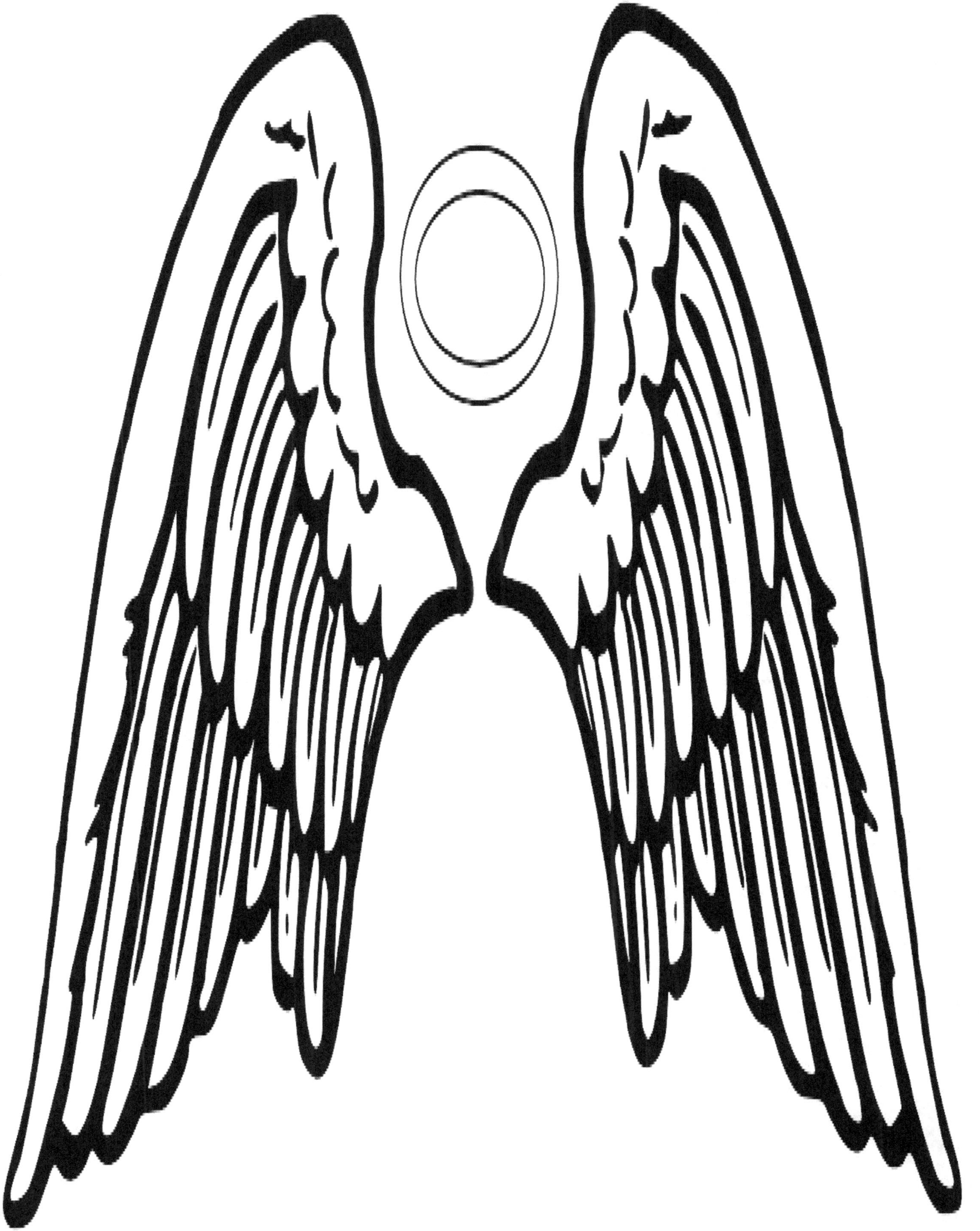

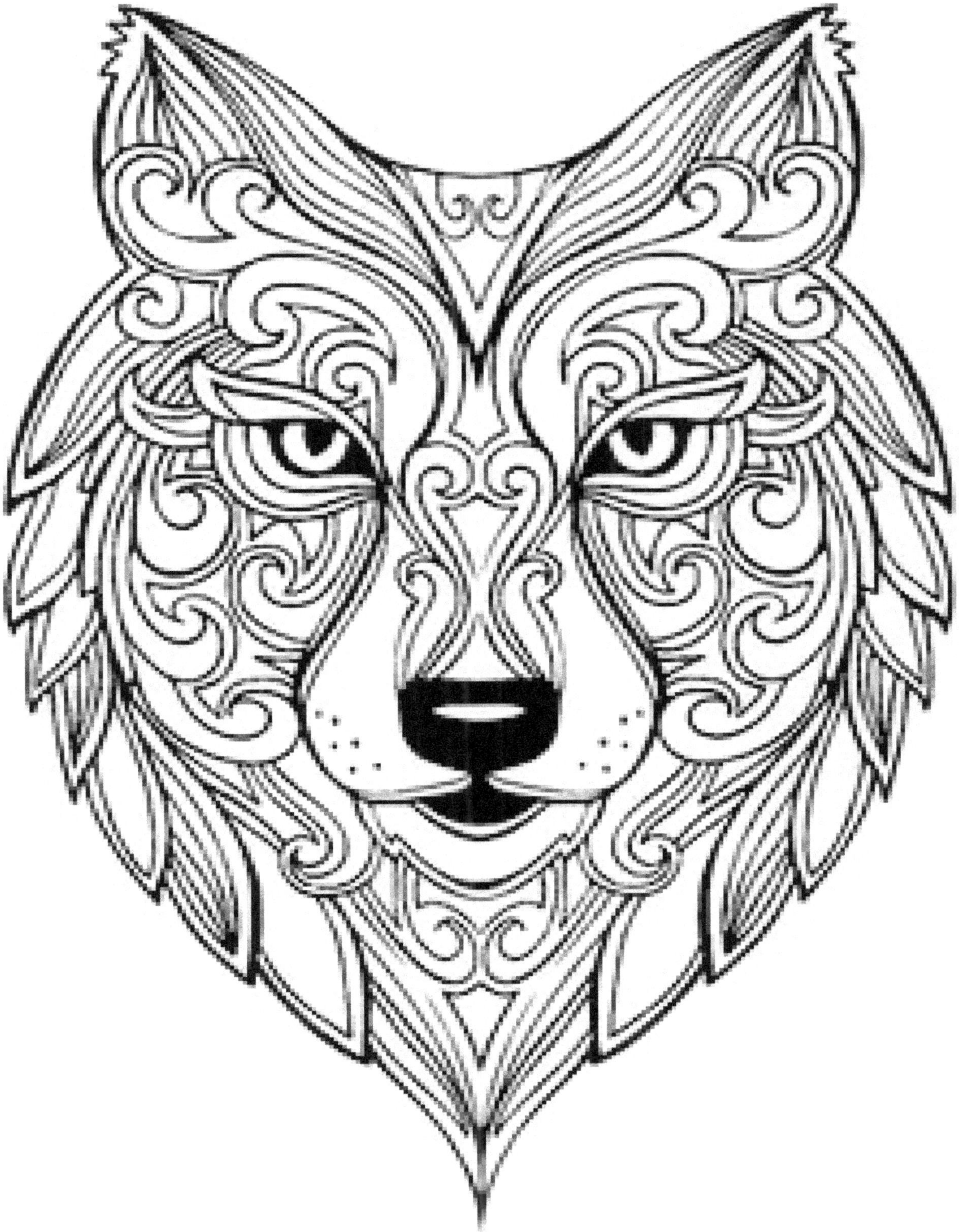

www.ingramcontent.com/pod-product-compliance
Lightning Source LLC
Chambersburg PA
CBHW080609220526
45466CB00010B/3297
9798588064699